First World War
and Army of Occupation
War Diary
France, Belgium and Germany

GUARDS DIVISION
3 Guards Brigade
Guards Machine Gun Company
3 December 1915 - 28 February 1918

WO95/1224/2

The Naval & Military Press Ltd
www.nmarchive.com
Published in association with The National Archives

Published by

The Naval & Military Press Ltd

Unit 10 Ridgewood Industrial Park,

Uckfield, East Sussex,

TN22 5QE England

Tel: +44 (0) 1825 749494

www.naval-military-press.com

www.nmarchive.com

This diary has been reprinted in facsimile from the original. Any imperfections are inevitably reproduced and the quality may fall short of modern type and cartographic standards.

© **Crown Copyright**
Images reproduced by permission of The National Archives, London, England, 2015.

Contents

Document type	Place/Title	Date From	Date To
Heading	WO95/1224 3 Guards Bde Machine Gun Co. Dec 15-Feb 18		
Heading	3rd Guards Brigade Machine Gun Company. December 1915 To Feb 1918		
War Diary	Rouge Croix.	03/12/1915	03/12/1915
War Diary	Pont Du Hem.	04/12/1915	14/12/1915
War Diary	Marais Laventie	14/12/1915	30/12/1915
Heading	Guards Division. 3rd Gds Brigade. Machine Gun Company. Jan-Dec 1916.		
War Diary	Marais	01/01/1916	07/01/1916
War Diary	Pont Du Hem.	07/01/1916	25/01/1916
War Diary	Estaires	25/01/1916	25/01/1916
War Diary	La Gorgue	30/01/1916	30/01/1916
Heading	3 Guards Bde M. Gun Coy Feb Vol II.		
War Diary	Laventie	01/02/1916	15/02/1916
War Diary	Estaires	15/02/1916	16/02/1916
War Diary	Lestrem	16/02/1916	16/02/1916
War Diary	Beau Marias Camp.	16/02/1916	26/02/1916
War Diary	Bavinghove	26/02/1916	26/02/1916
War Diary	Rictveld.	26/02/1916	26/02/1916
Heading	3 Guards Bde M Gun Coy Vol IV.		
War Diary	Rictveld.	06/03/1916	06/03/1916
War Diary	Watou	06/03/1916	13/03/1916
War Diary	Vlamertinge	13/03/1916	14/03/1916
War Diary	Ypres.	14/03/1916	26/03/1916
War Diary	Hazebrouck	26/03/1916	26/03/1916
War Diary	Brandhoek.	03/04/1916	03/04/1916
War Diary	Ypres.	03/04/1916	19/04/1916
War Diary	Brandhoek.	19/04/1916	26/04/1916
War Diary	Ypres	27/04/1916	27/04/1916
War Diary	Herzeele	01/06/1916	01/06/1916
War Diary	Houtkerque	01/06/1916	08/06/1916
War Diary	Herzeele	08/06/1916	16/06/1916
War Diary	Oosthoek	16/06/1916	17/06/1916
War Diary	Ypres	17/06/1916	06/07/1916
War Diary	Oosthoek	07/07/1916	14/07/1916
War Diary	Ypres	14/07/1916	26/07/1916
War Diary	Oosthoek	27/07/1916	27/07/1916
War Diary	Wulverdinghe	27/07/1916	29/07/1916
War Diary	Bavinchove	30/07/1916	30/07/1916
War Diary	St. Frevent	30/07/1916	30/07/1916
War Diary	Halloy	30/07/1916	30/07/1916
Heading	3rd Guards Brigade Guards Division. 3rd Guards Brigade. Machine Gun Company August 1916.		
War Diary	Halloy	01/08/1916	01/08/1916
War Diary	Bus-Les-Artois	01/08/1916	10/08/1916
War Diary	Mailly-Maillet	10/08/1916	19/08/1916
War Diary	Bus-Les-Artois	19/08/1916	20/08/1916
War Diary	Vauchelles	20/08/1916	22/08/1916
War Diary	Gezaincourt	22/08/1916	24/08/1916

War Diary	Vignacourt	24/08/1916	25/08/1916
War Diary	Mericourt-L'Abbe.	25/08/1916	25/08/1916
War Diary	Treaux	25/08/1916	09/09/1916
War Diary	Montauban	10/09/1916	13/09/1916
War Diary	Happy Valley	13/09/1916	14/09/1916
War Diary	Trones Wood	15/09/1916	17/09/1916
War Diary	Zuarries	20/09/1916	20/09/1916
War Diary	Trones Wood	22/09/1916	29/09/1916
War Diary	Minden Post	29/09/1916	30/09/1916
War Diary	Fricourt	01/10/1916	01/10/1916
War Diary	Etrejust	01/10/1916	31/10/1916
War Diary	Belloy-St-Leonard.	01/11/1916	01/11/1916
War Diary	Etrejust.	08/11/1916	08/11/1916
War Diary	Breilly.	08/11/1916	09/11/1916
War Diary	Daours.	09/11/1916	10/11/1916
War Diary	Sand. Pits Meaulte.	10/11/1916	10/11/1916
War Diary	Etrejust.	10/11/1916	10/11/1916
War Diary	Sandpits Meaulte	10/11/1916	14/11/1916
War Diary	Mansell Camp.	14/11/1916	21/11/1916
War Diary	Meaulte.	21/11/1916	01/12/1916
War Diary	Maltzhorn Fm	01/12/1916	01/12/1916
War Diary	Meaulte	02/12/1916	02/12/1916
War Diary	Maltzhorn Fm	02/12/1916	10/12/1916
War Diary	Mansel Camp	10/12/1916	10/12/1916
War Diary	Maltzhorn Fm	10/12/1916	10/12/1916
War Diary	Mansel Camp	11/12/1916	14/12/1916
War Diary	Maltzhorn Fm	14/12/1916	14/12/1916
War Diary	Combles & Haie Wood	22/12/1916	22/12/1916
War Diary	Bronfay	23/12/1916	27/12/1916
War Diary	Maltzhorn Fm	27/12/1916	27/12/1916
Miscellaneous	Mansell Camp Minden Post.		
Heading	Guards Division. 3rd Gds Brigade Machine Gun Coy. Jan-Dec 1917.		
War Diary	Maltzhorn Farm	01/01/1917	01/01/1917
War Diary	Bronfay Farm	01/01/1917	01/01/1917
War Diary	Haie Wood	01/01/1917	01/01/1917
War Diary	Trones Wood Siding	01/01/1917	01/01/1917
War Diary	Plateau Siding	02/01/1917	02/01/1917
War Diary	Bronfay Farm	02/01/1917	03/01/1917
War Diary	Treux	03/01/1917	10/01/1917
War Diary	Billon Farm	10/01/1917	24/01/1917
War Diary	Maurepas	24/01/1917	24/01/1917
War Diary	Fregicourt	24/01/1917	24/01/1917
War Diary	Combles	24/01/1917	24/01/1917
War Diary	Billon Farm	26/01/1917	26/01/1917
War Diary	Maurepas	26/01/1917	29/01/1917
War Diary	Fregicourt	29/01/1917	01/02/1917
War Diary	Maurepas	02/02/1917	02/02/1917
War Diary	Fregicourt	02/02/1917	02/02/1917
War Diary	Maurepas	06/02/1917	06/02/1917
War Diary	Fregicourt	06/02/1917	06/02/1917
War Diary	Sailly Sallisel	08/02/1917	08/02/1917
War Diary	Fregicourt	10/02/1917	10/02/1917
War Diary	Maurepas	10/02/1917	11/02/1917
War Diary	Plateau Siding	11/02/1917	11/02/1917
War Diary	Meaulte	11/02/1917	11/02/1917

War Diary	Treux		11/02/1917	11/02/1917
War Diary	Maurepas		11/02/1917	11/02/1917
War Diary	Treux		11/02/1917	20/02/1917
War Diary	Ville-Sur-Corbie		23/02/1917	23/02/1917
War Diary	Treux		01/03/1917	01/03/1917
War Diary	Billon		01/03/1917	02/03/1917
War Diary	Maurepas		02/03/1917	03/03/1917
War Diary	Haie Wood		03/03/1917	03/03/1917
War Diary	Sailly Sallisel		03/03/1917	03/03/1917
War Diary	Haie Wood		12/03/1917	12/03/1917
War Diary	Billon		12/03/1917	12/03/1917
War Diary	Haie Wood		12/03/1917	13/03/1917
War Diary	Maurepas		13/03/1917	13/03/1917
War Diary	Billon		13/03/1917	17/03/1917
War Diary	Maurepas		17/03/1917	18/03/1917
War Diary	Fregicourt		18/03/1917	21/03/1917
War Diary	St. Pierre Vaast		22/03/1917	24/03/1917
War Diary	Maurepas		24/03/1917	26/03/1917
War Diary	Le Transloy		26/03/1917	16/04/1917
War Diary	Halle		16/04/1917	03/05/1917
War Diary	Brusle		03/05/1917	18/05/1917
War Diary	Billon Camp		18/05/1917	19/05/1917
War Diary	Corbie		19/05/1917	30/05/1917
War Diary	St Omer		30/05/1917	30/05/1917
War Diary	Campagne		31/05/1917	17/06/1917
War Diary	Winnezeele		17/06/1917	18/06/1917
War Diary	Houtkerque		18/06/1917	02/07/1917
War Diary	Peselhoek		02/07/1917	02/07/1917
War Diary	Copper Nollehoek		02/07/1917	09/07/1917
War Diary	Forest Camp.		17/07/1917	17/07/1917
War Diary	Boesinghe		17/07/1917	17/07/1917
War Diary	Forest Camp		18/07/1917	18/07/1917
War Diary	Boesinghe		18/07/1917	18/07/1917
War Diary	Forest Camp		19/07/1917	19/07/1917
War Diary	Boesinghe		19/07/1917	19/07/1917
War Diary	Forest Camp		20/07/1917	20/07/1917
War Diary	Boesinghe		20/07/1917	21/07/1917
War Diary	Forest Camp		21/07/1917	21/07/1917
War Diary	Boesinghe		21/07/1917	21/07/1917
War Diary	Forest Camp		22/07/1917	22/07/1917
War Diary	Boesinghe		22/07/1917	23/07/1917
War Diary	Forest Camp		23/07/1917	23/07/1917
War Diary	Boesinghe		23/07/1917	23/07/1917
War Diary	Forest Camp		24/07/1917	24/07/1917
War Diary	Boesinghe		24/07/1917	25/07/1917
War Diary	Forest Camp		25/07/1917	25/07/1917
War Diary	Boesinghe		25/07/1917	26/07/1917
War Diary	Forest Camp		26/07/1917	26/07/1917
War Diary	Boesinghe		26/07/1917	26/07/1917
War Diary	Forest Camp		27/07/1917	27/07/1917
War Diary	Boesinghe		27/07/1917	27/07/1917
War Diary	Forest Camp		27/07/1917	27/07/1917
War Diary	Boesinghe		27/07/1917	28/07/1917
War Diary	Forest Camp		28/07/1917	28/07/1917
War Diary	Boesinghe		29/07/1917	31/07/1917
War Diary	Forest Camp.		01/08/1917	06/08/1917

War Diary	Boesinghe	07/08/1917	07/08/1917
War Diary	Forest Camp	07/08/1917	07/08/1917
War Diary	Plaistow Camp	07/08/1917	26/08/1917
War Diary	Ballantine Forest	26/08/1917	27/08/1917
War Diary	Langemarck	27/08/1917	28/08/1917
War Diary	Ballantine Forest	28/08/1917	30/08/1917
War Diary	Langemarck	30/08/1917	30/08/1917
War Diary	Ballantine Forest	31/08/1917	31/08/1917
War Diary	Langemarck.	31/08/1917	31/08/1917
Miscellaneous	App. 31		
Map	Langemarck		
War Diary	Forest Camp	01/09/1917	01/09/1917
War Diary	Langemarck	01/09/1917	01/09/1917
War Diary	Forest Camp	02/09/1917	02/09/1917
War Diary	Langemarck	02/09/1917	02/09/1917
War Diary	Forest Camp	03/09/1917	05/09/1917
War Diary	Langemarck	05/09/1917	05/09/1917
War Diary	Forest Camp	06/09/1917	13/09/1917
War Diary	Wellington Camp	13/09/1917	20/09/1917
War Diary	Point Camp	20/09/1917	21/09/1917
War Diary	Herzeele	21/09/1917	29/09/1917
War Diary	Plaistow Camp	29/09/1917	06/10/1917
War Diary	Elverdinghe	06/10/1917	06/10/1917
War Diary	Wellington Camp	06/10/1917	08/10/1917
War Diary	Broembeek	09/10/1917	09/10/1917
War Diary	Wellington Camp	09/10/1917	09/10/1917
War Diary	Burke Camp	09/10/1917	11/10/1917
War Diary	Broembeek.	11/10/1917	15/10/1917
War Diary	Burke Camp	15/10/1917	17/10/1917
War Diary	Pegwell Camp	17/10/1917	20/10/1917
War Diary	Proven Station	20/10/1917	20/10/1917
War Diary	St. Omer	20/10/1917	20/10/1917
War Diary	Owerstel	20/10/1917	25/10/1917
War Diary	Ouest Mont	25/10/1917	09/11/1917
War Diary	Serny	09/11/1917	10/11/1917
War Diary	Livossart	10/11/1917	11/11/1917
War Diary	Herlin-Le-Sec	11/11/1917	17/11/1917
War Diary	Oppy	17/11/1917	18/11/1917
War Diary	Bienvillers-Au-Bois.	18/11/1917	19/11/1917
War Diary	Achiet-Le-Petit	19/11/1917	22/11/1917
War Diary	Rocquigny	22/11/1917	23/11/1917
War Diary	Beaumetz	23/11/1917	23/11/1917
War Diary	Flesquieres	24/11/1917	24/11/1917
War Diary	Beaumetz	24/11/1917	24/11/1917
War Diary	Flesquieres	24/11/1917	24/11/1917
War Diary	Bourlon Sector	24/11/1917	29/11/1917
War Diary	Flesquieres	29/11/1917	29/11/1917
War Diary	Metz-En-Couture	30/11/1917	30/11/1917
War Diary	Gouzecourt Sector	01/12/1917	03/12/1917
War Diary	Metz-En-Couture	04/12/1917	04/12/1917
War Diary	Etricourt	05/12/1917	05/12/1917
War Diary	Saulty	05/12/1917	05/12/1917
War Diary	Barly	05/12/1917	05/12/1917
War Diary	Beaulencourt	05/12/1917	06/12/1917
War Diary	Barly	06/12/1917	11/12/1917
War Diary	Arras.	11/12/1917	31/12/1917

Heading	B.E.F. Guards Div 3 Gds Bde 3 Gds Bde Machine Gun Coy 1915 Dec to 1918 Feb.		
War Diary	Arras	01/01/1918	01/01/1918
War Diary	St. Nicholas	01/01/1918	18/01/1918
War Diary	Arras	18/01/1918	26/01/1918
War Diary	St. Nicholas	27/01/1918	06/02/1918
War Diary	Arras	06/02/1918	28/02/1918
Heading	Guards Division 3rd Gds Brigade Machine Gun Coy. Jan-Dec 1917.		

(2)

WO 95/1224

3 Guards Bde Machine Gun Co.

Dec 15 - Feb 18

WAR DIARY

3rd GUARDS BRIGADE MACHINE GUN COMPANY.

DECEMBER

1915

to Feb. 1918

WAR DIARY
INTELLIGENCE SUMMARY
(Erase heading not required.)

Army Form C. 2118

Sheet No. 1

Place	Date	Hour	Summary of Events and Information	Remarks and references to Appendices
			Machine Gun Company.	
			3rd Guards Bde.	
			For the month of December 1915.	
ROUGE CROIX	3/12	3.30pm	M.G. Conference at Div. S.Q. to fix the emplacements to be occupied permanently in the section of defence held by the Division.	
POINT DU HEM	4/12		Very windy and roads very dirty.	
	5/12	6.30am	Relieving teams paraded ready for trenches.	
	6/12		Sergt L.C. McEllison wounded slightly, still carried on with his duty.	
	7/12		Relieving teams paraded for trenches.	
	8/12		Relieving teams paraded for trenches.	
	9/12	6.30am	Co. paraded for rest billets remaining sections to move off when relieved	
			Regt and Guards Bde. Machine Gun Coy.	
MARAIS	10/12		Co. arrived at rest billets.	
LAVENTIE	11-13/12		Coys went into trenches.	
	14/12		Teams in front line relieved.	
	25/12		Teams in front line relieved.	
	28/12		Teams in front line relieved.	
	31/12		Teams in front line relieved.	

B.M.Y. Capt.
Commanding Machine Gun Coy.
3rd Guards Bde.

Guards Division.
3rd Gds Brigade.
Machine Gun Company.
Jan - Dec 1916.

Army Form C. 2118

WAR DIARY
INTELLIGENCE SUMMARY
(Erase heading not required.)

Sheet No. 1.

Instructions regarding War Diaries and Intelligence Summaries are contained in F. S. Regs., Part II. and the Staff Manual respectively. Title Pages will be prepared in manuscript.

Place	Date	Hour	Summary of Events and Information	Remarks and references to Appendices
			Machine Gun Company 3rd Guards Brigade. for the month of January 1916.	
MARAIS	1/16		Arrived at rest billets for the Coy.	
" "	6/16	1.15 a.m.	Coy left rest billets for trenches.	
PONT DU HEM	9/16	3 p.m.	Coy arrived 3 Guns went into front line trenches.	
	13/16	11.45 a.m.	Reliefs handed for trenches.	
	15/16		Reliefs paraded for trenches, accompanied by a detachment of 19th Welsh Coy.	
	16/16	11 a.m.	Church Service in billets.	
	17/16	11.45 a.m.	Reliefs paraded for trenches.	
	19/16		Reliefs paraded for trenches.	
	21/16		Reliefs paraded for trenches.	
	23/16		Reliefs paraded for trenches.	
	25/16	11 a.m.	Guns in front line relieved by 1st Guards Bde & marched back to rest billets.	
ESTAIRES	25/16	4 p.m.	Arrived in rest billets.	
LA GORGUE	30/16	quietly	Coy attended Divine Service.	

Buy Cass
Comdg Machine Gun Coy
3rd Guards Bde

3 Guards Bde
M Gun Coy

Feb

Vol XII

WAR DIARY
or
INTELLIGENCE SUMMARY
(Erase heading not required.)

Army Form C. 2118

Sheet No. 1

Place	Date	Hour	Summary of Events and Information	Remarks and references to Appendices
			Machine Gun Company	
			3rd Guards Bde.	
			For the month of February 1916	
LAVENTIE	1/2/16	6.30am	Company arrived 13 Guns went into trenches	
	15/2/16	5.15am	Company to stand to, move off, relieved by 23rd Brigade Machine Gun Coy.	
ESTAIRES	15/2/16	6.30am	Company arrived in billets.	
"	16/2/16	2.30am	Company left for station to entrain.	
LESTREM	16/2/16	8am	Company machine gunners left station.	
BEAU MARIAS CAMP		5.30am	Company arrived in Rest Camp.	
"	28/2/16	11.15am	Company left camp for station to entrain.	
BAVINCHOVE		1pm	Arrived at station.	
RIETVELD		11.30pm	Company arrived in Rest Billets.	

Bury Capt.
Comdg Machine Gun Coy.
3rd Guards Bde.

3 Guards Bde
M Gun Coy
Vol IV

Army Form C. 2118.

WAR DIARY
~~INTELLIGENCE~~ SUMMARY.
(Erase heading not required.)

Instructions regarding War Diaries and Intelligence Summaries are contained in F. S. Regs., Part II. and the Staff Manual respectively. Title pages will be prepared in manuscript.

Ypres

Machine Gun Company
3rd Guards Bde.
For the month of March 1916.

Place	Date	Hour	Summary of Events and Information	Remarks and references to Appendices
RIDGEFIELD	6/3/16	6.15am	Company paraded ready to move off.	
WATOU	6/3/16	11 a.m	Company arrived in billets.	
WATOU	13/3/16	4.30pm	Company paraded ready to move off.	
VLAMERTINGHE	13/3/16	6 p.m.	Arrived in Rest Subs.	
MARKETINGHE	14/3/16	8.45pm	Part of Company paraded ready to move off. Remainder left behind in camp.	
YPRES	14/3/16	9.30pm	Relief arrived to relieve the Machine Gun Coy of the 6th Bde.	
YPRES	21/3/16	9.30pm	Coy relieved by 2nd Gds Bde Machine Gun Coy. Teams from trenches brought down to billets in motor buses.	
HAZEBROUCK	21/3/16	11.45pm	Arrived in Rest Bets.	

BVM Capt.
Cmdg Machine Gun Coy.
3rd Guards Bde.

Army Form C. 2118.

WAR DIARY
of
INTELLIGENCE SUMMARY.
(Erase heading not required.)

Instructions regarding War Diaries and Intelligence Summaries are contained in F. S. Regs., Part II. and the Staff Manual respectively. Title pages will be prepared in manuscript.

Machine Gun Company.
3rd Guards Bde.
For the month of April 1916.

Place	Date	Hour	Summary of Events and Information	Remarks and references to Appendices
BRANDHOEK	3/4/16	6.50 am	Company paraded ready to move off.	
YPRES	3/4/16	10 am	Company arrived and relieved the Machine Gun Coy 1st Guards Bde.	
YPRES	19/4/16	1 am	Company relieved by Machine Gun Coy 2nd Guards Bde.	
BRANDHOEK	19/4/16	4 am	Company arrived in Rest Bro.	
BRANDHOEK	26/4/16	10.30 pm	Company moved off.	
YPRES	27/4/16	1 am	Company relieved Machine Gun Coy, 1st Guards Bde.	

L.B. Vinchilan 2nd Lieut.
Comdg Machine Gun Coy.
3rd Guards Bde.

3 Gds M.G. Coy
Army Form C. 2118.

WAR DIARY
or
INTELLIGENCE SUMMARY.
(Erase heading not required.)

Instructions regarding War Diaries and Intelligence Summaries are contained in F.S. Regs., Part II. and the Staff Manual respectively. Title pages will be prepared in manuscript.

Machine Gun Company
3rd Guards Brigade
For the month of June 1916

Place	Date	Hour	Summary of Events and Information	Remarks and references to Appendices
HERZEELE	1.6.16	3.30	Company formed & ready to move off	
HOUTKERQUE	1.6.16	30.30	Company arrived in Billets	
—	8.6.16	9.30	Company paraded ready to move off	
HERZEELE	8.6.16		Company arrived in Billets	
—	11.6.16	3.30	Company paraded ready to move off	
COSMOEK	11.6.16	12.11	Company arrived in Rest Area	
—	11.6.16		Company left to relieve 71st Brigade M.G. Coy and half of 76th Brigade M.G. Coy	
YPRES	11.6.16		Company proceeded to relieve 71st Brigade M.G. Coy and half of 76th Bde M.G. Coy	

B W Gapston
Captain,
Commanding Machine Gun Company
3rd Guards Brig.

Army Form C. 2118.

WAR DIARY
INTELLIGENCE SUMMARY.
(Erase heading not required.)

Vol 8

Instructions regarding War Diaries and Intelligence Summaries are contained in F. S. Regs., Part II. and the Staff Manual respectively. Title pages will be prepared in manuscript.

Machine Gun Company
3rd Guards Brigade
For the month of July 1916.

Place	Date	Hour	Summary of Events and Information	Remarks and references to Appendices
YPRES	6-7-16	10.30 P.M	Company relieved by 1st Gds Bde M.G. Coy.	
OOSTHOEK	7-7-16	1.0 A.M	Company arrived at Rest Huts.	
" "	14-7-16	8.0 P.M	Company moved off to relieve 2nd Gds. Bde. M.G. Coy	
YPRES	14-7-16	12. M	Company arrived to relieve 2nd Gds Bde. M.G. Coy	
" "	26-7-16	10 P.M	Company relieved by 11th Inf. Bde. M.G. Coy.	
OOSTHOEK	27-7-16	12.30 A.M	Company arrived at Rest Huts	
" "	27-7-16	7.45 A.M	Company paraded ready to move off. (Route via WORMHOUDT and BOLLEZEELE)	
HERZEELE	17-7-16	4.0 P.M	Company arrived in billets.	
" "	29-7-16	9.15 A.M	Company paraded ready to move off for station to entrain (Route via MENEGAT CROSS ROADS, NOORDPEENE and ZUDPEENE).	
INCHOVE	30-7-16	12.40 A.M	Arrived at Station.	
" "	30-7-16	3.50 A.M	Left Station	
PREVENT	30-7-16	4.55 A.M	Arrived at Station	
" "	30-7-16	20 A.M	Left Station for billets via BOUQUEMAISON	
" "	30-7-16	6 A.M	Company arrived in billets	

BM Kennedy Captain,
M.G. Coy,
3rd Gds Bde.

3rd Guards Brigade
Guards Division.

3rd Guards Brigade.

MACHINEGUN COMPANY

AUGUST 1 9 1 6

Army Form C. 2118.

WAR DIARY
of
INTELLIGENCE SUMMARY.
(Erase heading not required.)

Instructions regarding War Diaries and Intelligence Summaries are contained in F. S. Regs., Part II. and the Staff Manual respectively. Title pages will be prepared in manuscript.

Vol 9

Place	Date	Hour	Summary of Events and Information	Remarks and references to Appendices
			Machine Gun Company 3rd Guards Brigade	
			In the month of August 1916	
HALLOY	1-8-16	5.15 P	Company paraded ready to move off. Proceeded via THIEVRES and AUTHIE.	
BUS-LES-ARTOIS	1-8-16	9.0 P	Company arrived in camp.	
"	6-8-16		Company received 14 New Thread Light Guns to replace Vickers.	
"	10-8-16	0.9 P	Company paraded ready to move off to relieve the 2nd Inf. Bde. M. Gun Coy.	
			Proceeded via BERTRANCOURT and BEAUSSART.	
MAILLY-MAILLET	11-8-16	6.30 P	Company arrived to relieve 4th & 2nd Inf. Bde. M. Gun Coy.	
"	17-8-16	0.15 P	Company relieved by the 2nd Inf. Bde. M. Gun Coy.	
BUS-LES-ARTOIS	17-8-16	9.0 P	Company arrived in camp. Proceeded via BEAUSSART and BERTRANCOURT.	
"	20-8-16	0.9 P	Company paraded ready to move off. Proceeded via LOUVENCOURT.	
VAUCHELLES	20-8-16	2.30 P	Company arrived in billets.	
"	23-8-16	4.5 A	Company paraded ready to move off. Proceeded via SARTON.	
GEZAINCOURT	23-8-16	8.30 A	Company arrived in billets.	

Army Form C. 2118.

WAR DIARY
INTELLIGENCE SUMMARY.

Instructions regarding War Diaries and Intelligence Summaries are contained in F. S. Regs., Part II. and the Staff Manual respectively. Title pages will be prepared in manuscript.

Place	Date	Hour	Summary of Events and Information	Remarks and references to Appendices
GEZAINCOURT	24-8-16	9 A.M.	Company paraded ready to move off. Proceeded via LONGUEVILLETTE — CANDAS — CANAPLES ROAD.	
VIGNACOURT	24-8-16	3.0 P.M.	Company arrived and into billets at OLINCOURT CHATEAU.	
"	25-8-16	5.5 A.M.	Company paraded ready to move off.	
"	25-8-16	7.30 A.M.	Company moved to VIGNACOURT STATION and entrained.	
MERICOURT-L'ABBE.	25-8-16	3.30 P.M.	Company arrived at MERICOURT-L'ABBE STATION, detrained and moved off to billets.	
TREAUX	25-8-16	7 P.M.	Company arrived in billets.	

R. ...... Captain,
Commanding 711. Gun Coy.
3rd Guards Brigade.

Army Form C. 2118

WAR DIARY
or
INTELLIGENCE SUMMARY
(Erase heading not required.)

Vol 10

Instructions regarding War Diaries and Intelligence Summaries are contained in F. S. Regs., Part II. and the Staff Manual respectively. Title Pages will be prepared in manuscript.

Place	Date	Hour	Summary of Events and Information	Remarks and references to Appendices
			Machine Gun Company.	
			3rd Guards Bde.	
			For month of September 1916.	
TREUX	9/9/16	6 a.m.	Eight gun teams proceeded ready to move off. Proceeded by motor lorries via VILLE & CARNOY to relieve the 14th & 45th Infy. Bde. near GUINCHY	
		2.30 p.m.	Company less 2 teams proceeded ready to move off. Proceeded via VILLE & CARNOY to the QUARRIES near MONTAUBAN.	
MONTAUBAN	10/9/16	9.30 a.m.	2 gun teams proceeded to GUINCHY in support.	
	11/9/16	12 m.n.	6 gun teams relieved by 71st Infy. Bde. 3 guns returned by our own lorries.	
	12/9/16	12 m.n.	Company relieved by 1st & 2nd Guards Brigades, proceeded via CARNOY.	
HAPPY VALLEY	13/9/16	2 a.m.	Company arrived in camp.	
	14/9/16	6 p.m.	Company paraded ready to move off. Proceeded via CARNOY.	
TRONES WOOD	15/9/16		Company in new position. 7 guns proceeded to support the 1st & 2nd Guards Bde. 5 guns proceeded to the South of GUINCHY. 4 guns remained in TRONES WOOD.	
	16/9/16 night		Company relieved by the Machine Gun Coy. 20th div. in CARNOY.	
	17/9/16	10 a.m.	Company marched to QUARRIES and then went into bivouac.	
QUARRIES	20/9/16	7 p.m.	Company paraded ready to march off. Proceeded via MONTAUBAN to TRONES WOOD. 6 guns attached to their respective battalions proceeded to relieve the 59th Infy. Bde. Company less 6 guns proceeded via TRONES WOOD.	

Army Form C. 2118

WAR DIARY
or
INTELLIGENCE SUMMARY
(Erase heading not required.)

Events (2)

Instructions regarding War Diaries and Intelligence Summaries are contained in F. S. Regs., Part II. and the Staff Manual respectively. Title Pages will be prepared in manuscript.

Place	Date	Hour	Summary of Events and Information	Remarks and references to Appendices
TRONES WOOD	22/9/16	6.30pm	The 6 guns on the line relieved, the relieved teams staying in TRONES WOOD with remainder of company.	
"	24/9/16		Relief provided for the 6 guns on the trenches. 6pm – 6.30pm & 12 m.n.	
"	25/9/16	12 noon	8 guns attacked to the assaulting battalions, attacked and captured LESBOEUFS. 4 guns which returned to reconnoitre the captured positions during the night.	
"	26/9/16		During the night 26(2)nd Sept. Company relieved by the 2nd Guards Bde M.G.C.	
"	27/9/16		Company in bivouac at TRONES WOOD	
"	28/9/16	2pm	Company paraded and marched via CARNOY to MINDEN POST.	
MINDEN POST	29/9/16	5pm	Company arrived in camp.	
"	30/9/16	2pm	Company paraded and marched to rest camp south of FRICOURT arriving 3.30pm. Transport paraded ready to march off at 8.30am moved off via CORBIE to DAOURS.	

Bampt.
Company Machine Gun Coy.
3rd Guards Bde.

WAR DIARY or INTELLIGENCE SUMMARY

Army Form C. 2118

Vol XI

Machine Gun Company
3rd Guards Brigade
For month of October 1916

Place	Date	Hour	Summary of Events and Information	Remarks and references to Appendices
TRICOURT	1-10-16	8.30 am	Company paraded ready to move off from Camp South of TRICOURT. Marched cross-country to near MORLANCOURT, and from there travelled by Motor Busses via CORBIE, AMIENS, and TERRIERES.	
ETREJUST	1-10-16	6.0 pm	Arrived in billets.	
"	2-10-16	12 noon	Transport arrived in billets. Proceeded via DAOURS and AILLY.	
"	3-10-16 to 11-10-16		Company attended rehearsal of the inspection by Field Marshal H.R.H. The Duke of Connaught. The list of those who were presented to the following:-	

No 15610 C.S.M. W.A. Dobson (Military Medal)
No 7340 L.Q.M.S. P. Nesbit (Military Medal)
" 2699 Sergt. E. Roy A. (D.C.M + Military Medal) " 4191 L./Sgt. L. Gould (Military Medal)
" 5585 (Cpl) E. Lane (D.C.M.) " 15796 L./Cpl. W. Tilley (Military Medal)
" 1308 Pte E. Nelson (Military Medal) " 7305 Pte A. Bowling (Military Medal)
" 3034 Pte T. Rose (Military Medal) " 7972 Pte A.E. Page (Military Medal)
" 7501 " R. Morrison (Military Medal)

Capt. Shalwood J. (D.C.M.) unable to be on parade
owing to sickness

B.M. ?? Captain
Comdg M.G. Company
3rd Gds Bde

WAR DIARY
INTELLIGENCE SUMMARY

Army Form C. 2118

3 Gds Bn M G Coy

Machine Gun Company
3rd Guards Brigade
1st month of November 1916.

Place	Date	Hour	Summary of Events and Information	Remarks and references to Appendices
ELLOY-ST. EONARD.	1-11-16	10.0 A.M	Company attended Inspection of Guards Division by Field Marshal H.R.H. The Duke of Connaught.	
TREJUST.	8-11-16	8.0 A.M	Transport paraded ready to move off by road. Proceeded via METIGNY, AIRAINES, SOUES, and PICQUIGNY.	
BREILLY.	8-11-16	8.30 P.M	Transport arrived and stopped there for the night 8th/9th	
— do —	9-11-16	7.0 A.M	Transport moved off. Proceeded via AILLY-SUR-SOMME and AMIENS.	
DAOURS.	"	6.0 P.M	Transport arrived and stopped there for the night 9th/10th.	
— do —	10-11-16	7.0 A.M	Transport moved off. Proceeded via CORBIE.	
SANDPITS MEAULTE	10-11-16	10.0 E.M	Transport arrived in Camp.	
ETRE JUST.	"	8.45 A.M	Company (less Transport) marched to ST. MAULVIS, and from there proceeded by Motor Busses via AIRAINES, AILLY-SUR-SOMME, AMIENS and CORBIE.	
SANDPITS MEAULTE.	"	5.0 P.M	Company (less Transport) arrived in Camp.	The weather condition was very bad during this first stay in the trenches
— do —	13-11-16	10.0 A.M	8 Teams moved off to trenches relieving 8 of the 51st & 52nd Infantry Brigade M.Gun Companies.	
— do —	14-11-16	9.0 A.M	Company paraded ready to move off. Proceeded via FRICOURT.	
MANSELL CAMP.	"	11.0 A.M	Company arrived in Camp. Q.M. Stores and Transport proceeded to MONTAUBAN to be quartered.	
— do —	15-11-16	12 noon	Remaining 8 Teams proceeded to trenches to complete relief.	
— do —	21-11-16	9.0 A.M	Company paraded ready to move off after being relieved by 15th Australian M.G. Coy. Proceeded via FRICOURT followed an hour later by the Transport and Q.M. Stores from MONTAUBAN.	
MEAULTE.	"	12 noon	Company arrived in billets.	

Sm?
Captain,
Comdg. M. Gun Company,
3rd Guards Brigade

WAR DIARY or INTELLIGENCE SUMMARY

Army Form C. 2118

3 Gds M Gy Coy Vol/3

Machine Gun Company
3rd Guards Brigade
For month of December 1916

Place	Date	Hour	Summary of Events and Information	Remarks and references to Appendices
MEAULTE	1-12-16	12 noon	2 Sections (4th & Grenadiers & 2nd Scots Guards) moved off to MALTZHORN FARM.	
MALTZHORN FM	1-12-16	4.30 P.M.	Above Sections arrived and took over bell tents from the French.	
MEAULTE	2-12-16	12 noon	Company (less above 2 Sections) moved off to MALTZHORN FARM.	
MALTZHORN FM	2-12-16	5.0 P.M.	Company arrived.	
do	3-12-16		2 Sections (4 Grenadiers & Scots Guards) moved off to relieve Machine Guns of the 296th and 125th French Regiments. 8 guns relieving 16 on SAILLY SAILLISEL front.	
do	6-12-16	2.15 P.M.	1st Grenadiers & 1st Welsh Guards Sections paraded and moved off to relieve the 2 Sections on the line. Company headquarters established at CATACOMBS, COMBLES.	
MANSEL CAMP	10-12-16	12 noon	Company (less 2 Sections in line) paraded, ready to move off.	
MALTZHORN FM	10-12-16	2.30 P.M.	Company arrived and took over huts.	
MANSEL CAMP	11-12-16	12 noon	The 2 Sections returned, after being relieved by Machine Guns of 5th Australian Divn. The 2 Sections arrived at MANSEL CAMP off(?) having been accommodated 1 night at MALTZHORN FM.	
do	13-12-16	1.30 P.M.	2 Sections (1st Grenadiers and Welsh Guards) moved off to MALTZHORN FARM.	
do	14-12-16	1.30 P.M.	Company (less 1st Grenadiers & Welsh Guards) moved off to COMBLES and HAIE WOOD. 1st Grenadiers and Welsh Guards Sections moved off to relieve Machine Guns of the 1st Guards Brigade Machine Gun Company. Company Headquarters at HAIE WOOD.	
MALTZHORN FM	14-12-16	1.0 P.M.	Q.M. Stores and Transport billeted at MARICOURT CHATEAU.	
COMBLES + HAIE WOOD	22-12-16	12 noon	Company relieved by 1st Guards Brigade Machine Gun Company.	
BRONFAY	23-12-16	2 noon(?)	Company arrived in huts at CAMP 108 BRONFAY.	
do	26-12-16	2.0 P.M.	2 Section (1st Grenadiers & Welsh Gds) paraded and moved off to MALTZHORN FARM.	
do	27-12-16	1.30 P.M.	Company (less above Section) paraded, moved off to MALTZHORN FARM.	
MALTZHORN FM	27-12-16	1.0 P.M.	1st Grenadiers & Welsh Gds Section moved off to HAIE WOOD and found 11 guns to relieve the 1st Gds Bde M. Gun Coy. Coy H.Q. & 2nd Scots Gds Section arrived at MALTZHORN FARM.	
do	27-12-16	3.0 P.M.	4th Gren Bn & Scots Gds Section arrived at MALTZHORN FARM.	R.T. Bury Capt. Commanding 3 Gds Bde M Gn Coy

	MANSELL CAMP MINDEN POST.	"H" CAMP CARNOY MONTAUBAN-ROAD.	"P" CAMP MONTAUBAN.	"D" CAMP TRONES WOOD.	FRONT LINE RIGHT	FRONT LINE LEFT.
27th.	3rd Gren. Gds.	1st Scots Gds.	1st Gren. Gds.	1st Welsh Gds.	4th Gren. Gds.	2nd Scots Gds.
28th.	3rd Gren. Gds.	1st Scots Gds.	2nd Scots Gds.	1st Gren. Gds.	4th Gren. Gds.	1st Welsh Gds.
29th.	3rd Gren. Gds.	1st Scots Gds.	2nd Scots Gds.	1st Gren. Gds.	4th Gren. Gds.	1st Welsh Gds.
30th.	3rd Gren. Gds.	4th Gren. Gds.	2nd Scots Gds.	1st Scots Gds.	1st Gren. Gds.	1st Welsh Gds.
DEC. 1st.	3rd Gren. Gds.	4th Gren. Gds.	2nd Scots Gds.	1st Scots Gds.	1st Gren. Gds.	1st Welsh Gds.
2nd.	1st Welsh Gds.	4th Gren. Gds.	2nd Scots Gds.	3rd Gren. Gds.	1st Gren. Gds.	1st Scots Gds.
3rd.	1st Welsh Gds.	4th Gren. Gds.	2nd Scots Gds.	3rd Gren. Gds.	1st Gren. Gds.	1st Scots Gds.
4th.	1st Welsh Gds.	4th Gren. Gds.	1st Gren. Gds.	2nd Scots Gds.	3rd Gren. Gds.	1st Scots Gds.
5th.	1st Welsh Gds.	4th Gren. Gds.	1st Gren. Gds.	2nd Scots Gds.	3rd Gren. Gds.	1st Scots Gds.
6th.	1st Welsh Gds.	1st Scots Gds.	1st Gren. Gds.	4th Gren. Gds.	3rd Gren. Gds.	2nd Scots Gds.

Guards Division.
3rd Gds Brigade
Machine Gun Coy.
Jan — Dec 1917.

Army Form C. 2118

WAR DIARY
INTELLIGENCE SUMMARY
(Erase heading not required.)

For Month of January 1917

Vol 14

Instructions regarding War Diaries and Intelligence Summaries are contained in F. S. Regs., Part II. and the Staff Manual respectively. Title Pages will be prepared in manuscript.

Machine Gun Company
3rd Guards Brigade

Place	Date	Hour	Summary of Events and Information	Remarks and references to Appendices
MALTZHORN FARM	1-1-17	10 noon	1st Grenadiers and M.G. Guards Sections found ready to move off.	
BRONFAY FARM	"	2.30 p.m.	Arrived in huts at CAMP 108 BRONFAY	
PINE WOOD	"	10. 0 p.m.	Company (less 1st Gren Gds & M.G. Gds Section) relieved partly by 52nd and 59th Inf. Bde M.Gun Companies	
"	"	"	Relief of 11 Guns Complete.	
TRÔNES WOOD SIDING	"	10.30 p.m.	Company paraded and moved off via MALTZHORN FARM	
PLATEAU SIDING	2-1-17	12.	Company (less above Sections) entrained for PLATEAU SIDING	
BRONFAY FARM	"	12.30 a.m.	Company arrived and moved off	
"	"	2. 0 a.m.	Company arrived in huts at CAMP 108 BRONFAY	
TREUX	3-1-17	10. 0 a.m.	Company paraded ready to move off to billets in VILLE AREA. Route via BRAY and MORLANCOURT.	
"	"	1.30 p.m.	Company arrived in billets	
"	10-1-17	9.30 a.m.	Company paraded and moved off. Route via VILLE, MEAULTE, LE CARCAILLOT, and BRAY.	
BILLON FARM	"	1. 0 p.m.	Company arrived in huts at CAMP 16	
"	20-1-17	8.45 a.m.	Company paraded and moved off	
"	"	10.30 a.m.	Company arrived and accommodation found in tents and dug-outs. Transport remained at BILLON FM.	
MAUREPAS	"	11.30 a.m.	Company paraded and moved off to relieve 2nd Gds Bde M Gun Company in the line.	
FREGICOURT	"	9.30 p.m.	Relief of 12 Guns Complete. 1st Battalion Welsh Guards Sections found 6 guns each.	
COMBLES	"	"	Company Headquarters at FREGICOURT.	
"	"	"	4 M Gun Sections and Scots Guards Sections taking billets from 2nd Gds Bde M. Gun Coy at COMBLES.	
BILLON FARM	21-1-17	7. 0 a.m.	Transport moved off	
MAUREPAS	"	10. 0 a.m.	Transport arrived and took over stables	
"	27-1-17	3. 0 p.m.	Teams for horses moved off to relieve the 1st Grenadier and Welsh Gds Sections in the line.	
			Guns were found from remainder of 4 M.G. sections and Scots Gds at MAUREPAS and comprised from above Sections at COMBLES.	
			Relief complete. Part of 1st Grenadiers and Welsh Gds Sections returned to COMBLES and remainder to MAUREPAS.	

Major
Commanding Machine Gun Company
3rd Guards Brigade

1875 Wt. W503/826 1,000,000 4/15 J.B.C. & A. A.D.S.S./Forms/C. 2118.

Army Form C. 2118

WAR DIARY
INTELLIGENCE SUMMARY
(Erase heading not required.)

For Month of February 1917

Vol 15

Place	Date	Hour	Summary of Events and Information	Remarks and references to Appendices
—	1/2/17	—	3rd Guards Machine Gun Company. From this date all Guards Machine Gun Companies administered as a Regiment from the Welsh Guards Orderly Room, Buckingham Gate, London, S.W.	
MAUREPAS	5/2/17	3.30 P.M.	Teams for trenches moved off to relieve the 4 Grenadier and Scots Guards Sections in the line.	
FREGICOURT	"	9.0 P.M.	Relief complete. Part of 4th Grenadiers and Scots Guards Sections returned to COMBLES and remainder to MAUREPAS.	
			Weather severely cold and frosty.	
MAUREPAS	6/2/17	3.30 P.M.	Teams for trenches moved off to relieve the 1st Grenadier and Welsh Guards Sections in the line.	
FREGICOURT	"	9.0 P.M.	Relief complete. Part of 1st Grenadiers and Welsh Guards Sections returned to COMBLES and remainder to MAUREPAS.	
			Weather severely cold and frosty.	
SAILLY SAILLISEL	8/2/17	7.30 P.M.	The 17th Division holding line on left of Guards Division carried out an attack on the enemy's trenches. The Machine Guns of 3rd Guards Machine Gun Company co-operated in the attack by forming barrages of fire.	
TREGICOURT	10/2/17	7.0 P.M.	Company relieved by the 1st Guards Machine Gun Company.	
MAUREPAS	"	8.0 P.M.	Relief complete. Teams from line and men at COMBLES and FREGICOURT returned to MAUREPAS.	
	11/2/17	9.15 A.M.	Company paraded and moved off to billets at TREUX.	
PLATEAU SIDING	"	11.30 A.M.	Company entrained for MEAULTE.	
MEAULTE	"	12.45 P.M.	Company arrived and detrained and moved off.	
TREUX	"	2.0 P.M.	Company arrived in billets.	
MAUREPAS	"	7.30 A.M.	Transport moved off, proceeding via MARICOURT, TRICOURT and MEAULTE.	
TREUX	"	12. noon	Transport arrived at billets.	
			Weather still very cold and frosty.	
	20/2/17		Weather much milder and thawing commences.	
VILLE-SUR-CORBIE	23/2/17	7.50 A.M.	The Company with guns and all equipment in limber paraded and attended an Inspection of the 3rd Guards Brigade by the French Minister of War.	

BWM Major
Commd'g 3rd Guards
Machine Gun Coy

WAR DIARY / INTELLIGENCE SUMMARY

Army Form C. 2118

March 1917

Place	Date	Hour	Summary of Events and Information	Remarks and references to Appendices
TREUX	1.3.17	11.50 a.m.	Company paraded and moved off with transport.	
BILLON	"	5.0 p.m.	Company arrived and rested the night in CAMP 16.	
"	2.3.17	9.40 a.m.	Company paraded and moved off.	
MAUREPAS	"	12 noon	Company arrived in Camp at MAUREPAS RAVINE.	
"	3.3.17	11.30 a.m.	Company paraded and moved off to relieve the 88th Inf. Bde. M. Gun Company on the Night and part of the 96th Inf. Bde. M. Gun Company on the left in the SAILLY SAILLISEL Sector. Transport and Q.M. Stores remained at MAUREPAS.	
HAIE WOOD	"	12.50 p.m.	Company arrived. Coy. Headquarters and reserve other ranks accommodate in dug-outs. Relief of 16 guns found for the line. Relief complete.	
SAILLY SAILLISEL	"	9.30 p.m.		
HAIE WOOD	12.3.17	4.45 p.m.	Company Headqrs and reserve other ranks paraded and moved off.	
BILLON	"	4.30 p.m.	Company Headqrs and reserve other ranks arrived in CAMP 16.	
HAIE WOOD	"	11.0 p.m.	Teams in the line relieved by 2nd Gds. Bde. M. Gun Coy	
"	13.3.17	1.0 a.m.	Relief Complete.	
"	"	1.30 a.m.	Teams paraded after being relieved and moved off to Camp at MAUREPAS RAVINE.	
MAUREPAS	"	3.0 a.m.	Teams arrive from HAIE WOOD and rested.	
"	"	12.30 p.m.	Teams moved off	
BILLON	"	2.30 p.m.	Teams arrive and accommodated with remainder of Company at CAMP 16.	
"	17.3.17	2.0 p.m.	Company and transport paraded and moved off. Surplus Kit and stores left at BRONFAY CAMP.	
MAUREPAS	"	4.30 p.m.	Company arrived and rested for the night in CAMP at MAUREPAS RAVINE.	
"	18.3.17	2.30 p.m.	Coy paraded and moved off to relieve the 2nd Gds. Bde. M. Gun Coy in the line (FREGICOURT Sector)	
FREGICOURT	"	5.0 p.m.	Coy Hdqrs. established at GUN PITS. E. of FREGICOURT on arrival. Transport & Q.M. Stores at MAUREPAS	
"	"	9.0 p.m.	Relief of 7th Guns in the line complete.	
"	19.3.17	-	1st & 2nd & 6 Gds Section accompanied the 1st Bn Grenadier Gds, who established an outpost line in front of HENNOIS WOOD. 4th Grenadier Guards section occupied line running through GOVERNMENT FM.	
"	24.3.17	-	Coy less 2 Sections moved forward to ST PIERRE VAAST WOOD near to GOVERNMENT FARM. 4th gds Grenadiers sect was relieved. 1 & 2 gren gds sections and occupied line in front of RIVERSIDE WD beyond MANANCOURT. 3rd rest. 4th gds relieved 4th Grenadier Gds in GOVERNMENT FM line.	
MAUREPAS	24.3.17	12 noon	Coy relieved by 25th Inf. Bde. M. Gun Coy and retired to CAMP at CAMP B.3 Central, MAUREPAS RAVINE.	
"	26.3.17	2 p.m.	Coy arrived and accommodated in dug-outs at CAMP B.3 Central, MAUREPAS RAVINE.	
LE TRANSLOY	27.3.17	5.30 p.m.	Company paraded and moved off via COMBLES, FREGICOURT, and SAILLY SAILLISEL. Company arrived and accommodated in tents. Transport & QM Stores at MAUREPAS.	
"	"	-	Company employed on fatigue work under C.R.E.	

W. Dagg Lieut.
Commanding 3rd Guards
Bde. M. Gun Company.

Army Form C. 2118.

WAR DIARY
INTELLIGENCE SUMMARY
(Erase heading not required.)

Machine Gun Company,
3rd Guards Brigade
For month of April 1917.

Vol 17

Place	Date	Hour	Summary of Events and Information	Remarks and references to Appendices
LE TRANSLOY	From 1-4-17 to 15-4-17	—	Company employed on labour, i.e. making roads and railways under supervision of C.R.E.	
do	16-4-17	12.30 p.m.	Company paraded and moved off to HALLE (I.9.b. ALBERT Combined Sheet). Route via MAUREPAS and CLERY.	
HALLE	do	5.0 p.m.	Company arrived. Accommodated in tents.	
do	17-4-17 to 30-4-17	—	Company engaged on a period of training in Coy. Drill and Machine Gun work. On 21-4-17 the Company was inspected by G.O.C. 3rd Guards Brigade.	

M.W.P. Captain,
Commanding 3rd Gds Bde M. Gun Coy.

WAR DIARY or INTELLIGENCE SUMMARY

Army Form C. 2118

3 Gds. Bde. M.G. Coy
Month of May 1917

Vol 18

Place	Date	Hour	Summary of Events and Information	Remarks and references to Appendices
HALLE	1-5-17	7.30 a.m.	3rd Guards Brigade M. Gun Coy. Company paraded for training in Company Drill, Physical Training and Gun Drill.	
"	2-5-17	9.0 a.m.	" " " " " " " " " " " " Indication and Recognition.	
"	3-5-17	1.0 p.m.	Company paraded together with Transport and moved by road to BRUSLE via PERONNE. All tents were moved and pitched at BRUSLE for accommodation of Company.	
BRUSLE	"	4.0 p.m.	Company arrived.	
"	4-5-17	8.0 a.m.	Company paraded for Company Drill and Camp Improvement.	
"	5-5-17	8.0 a.m.	Company paraded for Company Drill, Physical Training, Use of ground and Cover and a lecture for N.C.O's "Fire Direction".	
"	6-5-17	10.20 a.m.	Company attended Divine Service.	
"	7-5-17	8.0 a.m.	Company paraded for training as follows:- Company Drill, advanced Gun Drill, Indication and Recognition, and practice in Range-finding & Signalling for ships.	
"	8-5-17	7.30 a.m.	Company paraded for training as follows:- Company Drill, Lecture, Map reading and Gun Drill to work for Officers and N.C.O's, Physical Training & Gun Drill. All rifles were inspected by Armourer Sergeant.	
"	9-5-17	7.30 a.m.	Company paraded for training as follows:- Gas helmet and arm drill, advanced drill, and stoppages.	
			Lieut. Prince G. Imeretinsky rejoined Company from M.G.C Base Depot.	
"	10-5-17	7.30 a.m.	Company paraded for training as follows:- Company Drill, Immediate Action and Stoppages for 7 Section. Remaining 2 sections on Field Training.	
"	11-5-17	9 a.m.	Company paraded for a Field Day.	
"	12-5-17	7.15 a.m.	7 Section paraded for Field Day. Remainder of Coy engaged on Stoppages.	
			Gas Drill and Physical Training.	
"	13-5-17	8.30 a.m.	Company paraded and attended Divine Service.	
"	"	6.45 p.m.	1 Section on Field Day in Conjunction with scheme practiced by 1st Bn Grenadier Guards.	
"	14-5-17	8.0 a.m.	Company Drill and Physical Training. Headquarters, Transport and 3 sections inoculated this date.	

WAR DIARY or INTELLIGENCE SUMMARY

Army Form C. 2118

For Month of May 1917 (continued)

Place	Date	Hour	Summary of Events and Information	Remarks and references to Appendices
BRUSLE	15-5-17	7.45 P.M.	1 Section carried out Field Day in conjunction with Scheme practiced by 3rd Bn Cols Guards. Remainder of Coy resting after inoculation.	
"	16-5-17	10 A.M.	1 Section paraded and did Camp fatigue. Remainder of Company resting after inoculation. G.O.C. 3rd Guards Brigade inspected Camp and Transport.	
"	17-5-17	8.0 A.M.	Company paraded for training in Company Drill, Physical Training and Arm Drill.	
"	18-5-17	8.10 A.M.	Company paraded together with transport and moved by road to BILLON CAMP via PERONNE – CLERY – MARICOURT.	
BILLON CAMP	"	3.30 P.M.	Company arrived and accommodated in huts.	
"	19-5-17	1.15 P.M.	Company paraded with Transport and moved by road via BRAY to CORBIE.	
CORBIE	"	3.15 P.M.	Company arrived in billets at RUE DE MARAIS, CORBIE.	
"	20-5-17	9.0 A.M.	Company paraded and attended Divine Service.	
"	21-5-17	8.0 A.M.	Company paraded for training in Gas Drill, Arm Drill and Immediate Action.	
"	22-5-17	8.0 A.M.	Company paraded for training in Gas Drill, Immediate Action, Arms & Saluting Drill.	
"	"	4.15 P.M.	1 Section paraded for inoculation.	
"	23-5-17	4.5 A.M.	Company paraded (less 1 section resting after inoculation) for firing on Range (stoppages).	
"	24-5-17	4.5 P.M.	Company paraded for Baths and afterwards carried out training in Gun Drill and Elementary Training.	
"	25-5-17	8.0 A.M.	Company carried out firing practices on Range.	
"	26-5-17	8.30 A.M.	Company carried out Tactical Exercise under Brigade arrangements.	
"	27-5-17	10.0 A.M.	Company attended Divine Service.	
"	28-5-17	8.30 A.M.	Kit inspection for whole Company followed by Gas Drill & Arm Drill. All ranks handed in to Bn. D.O.T.	
"	29-5-17	3.30 P.M.	Company paraded and practiced coming into action from line of march also fire orders and Gas Drill.	
"	30-5-17	8.0 P.M.	Coy paraded (less 1 section transport paraded at 6.30 p.m.) & proceeded for loading purposes) and entrained at CORBIE STATION to proceed by rail to billets near ST OMER. Route via AMIENS–ABBEVILLE–BOULOGNE–CALAIS.	
ST OMER	"	7.30 P.M.	Coy arrived & to billets near CAMPAGNE.	
CAMPAGNE	31-5-17	9.30 A.M. 3 P.M.	Coy paraded and practised putting M.Guns in & back mules also gun drill.	

H. Neill. Captain
Commanding M Guin Coy
3rd Guards Bde.

WAR DIARY or INTELLIGENCE SUMMARY

Army Form C. 2118

3 Gds Bde M Gun Coy

For month of June 1917.

Vol 19

Place	Date	Hour	Summary of Events and Information	Remarks and references to Appendices

3rd Guards Brigade Machine Gun Company

Place	Date	Hour	Summary of Events and Information
CAMPAGNE	1-6-17	7.0 P.M.	Company paraded for Gas Drill, Arm Drill + Route March combined with coming into action from limbers on the march.
"	2-6-17	8.0 A.M.	Company paraded for Company Drill, Physical Training + Gun Drill. Lecture for NCOs on fire direction.
"	3-6-17	10.20 A.M.	Company paraded and attended Divine Service.
"	4-6-17	7.0 A.M.	Company paraded for Arm and Gas Drill followed by Route March + Bathing parade.
"	5-6-17	8.0 A.M.	Company paraded for Training in Fire Orders, Indication + Recognition + Gas Drill.
"	6-6-17	7.0 P.M.	Company paraded for Arm Drill.
"		10.0 A.M.	Transport inspected by Brigadier General + men inspected in Gas Drill.
"	7-6-17	8.0 P.M.	Company paraded for Arm Drill and Revolver Practice. Lieut. Vale & M. Babcock, Grenadier Guards awarded the Military Cross.
"	8-6-17	8.0 A.M.	Company paraded for a Route March. 2/Lieut A.H. Wilson, Scots Guards joined Company from M.G.C. (Base Depot).
"	9-6-17	8.0 A.M.	Company paraded for practice in Fire Orders and Indirect unobserved fire. also a lecture by C.O.
"	10-6-17	10.30 A.M.	Company paraded for Divine Service.
"	11-6-17	8 A.M.	Company paraded for cleaning Guns Kits. Gun Commanders practised Map reading and Lecture given on same subject by Section Officers. Practice also given in laying out a line of fire.
"	12-6-17	8. 0 A.M.	Company paraded for same work as 11th
"	13-6-17	8. 0 A.M.	Company paraded for indirect barrage of fire practice. Guns + kit being carried on pack animals. A lecture given team under Lt. Col. G. C. W. Ellison. M.C. attended at 4 Q.H. of Bn Grenadier Guards for instructional purposes.
"	14-6-17	8. 0 A.M.	Company paraded for training in Indication + Recognition and Range Cards.
"	15-6-17	7. 0 A.M.	Company paraded for a Route March.
"	16-6-17	8. 0 A.M.	Company paraded for Kit inspection, Arm Drill and Mechanism. 2 Lieut. J. Barnes, Grenadier Guards, admitted to hospital.

Army Form C. 2118.

WAR DIARY
INTELLIGENCE SUMMARY
(Erase heading not required.)

Month of June 1917 (Continued)

Place	Date	Hour	Summary of Events and Information	Remarks and references to Appendices
CAMPAGNE	17-6-17	7.0 A.M.	Company paraded together with Transport and moved off. Coy halted on the way from	2 & 4 & 5
WINNEZEELE		7.30 P.M.	Company arrived at LE TEMPLE near WINNEZEELE and bivouacked in a field for the night 17/18th. Route taken via ZUYTPEENE and WEMAERS-CAPPEL.	
"	18-6-17	3.45 P.M.	Company paraded and moved off to billets near HOUTKERQUE. Route taken via WINNEZEELE and DROGLANDT.	
HOUTKERQUE	---	6.0 P.M.	Company arrived in billets.	
"	19-6-17	9.0 A.M.	Company paraded for Box Respirator Drill and refilling belts.	
"	20-6-17	8.0 A.M.	2 sections paraded for overhauling gun-kit, ammunition & making dummies.	
"	"	5.50 P.M.	2 sections paraded and carried out digging work on Training Ground near HERZEELE	
"	21-6-17	5.40 A.M.	do	
"	"	2.40 P.M.	do	
"	22-6-17	5.40 A.M.	do	
"	"	9.0 A.M.	Sub section of 1st Grenadiers and 2nd Scots Guards paraded and moved off to training ground for practice attack with 4th Bn Grenadier Guards and 1st Bn Welsh Guards. Remaining sub sections paraded for emptying and refilling belts.	
"	23-6-17	15 A.M.	4 subsections paraded in fighting order and moved off to training ground for practice attack with Battalion.	
"	"	10.30 P.M.	Remainder of Company paraded and moved to new billets in XIV th Corps area West of HOUTKERQUE.	
"	"		Lt E.G.M. Ellison M.C. proceeded to Gds. Div. H.Qrs to learn Staff duties.	
"	24-6-17	7.30 A.M.	2 sections paraded in fighting order and moved off to Training Ground for practice attack.	
"	"	9.0 A.M.	Remaining 2 sections paraded for indirect fire practice.	
"	25-6-17	7.30 A.M.	2 sub sections paraded in fighting order and practiced attack with Battalion on Training Ground.	
"	"	9.0 A.M.	Remaining sections paraded for arm drill & gun drill.	
"	26-6-17	7.30 A.M.	2 sections paraded and moved off to Training Ground and carried out practice attack with Battalion.	

Army Form C. 2118

WAR DIARY
~~INTELLIGENCE SUMMARY~~

(Erase heading not required.)

For month of June 1917 (continued).

Instructions regarding War Diaries and Intelligence Summaries are contained in F. S. Regs., Part II. and the Staff Manual respectively. Title Pages will be prepared in manuscript.

Place	Date	Hour	Summary of Events and Information	Remarks and references to Appendices
HOUTKERQUE	26-6-17	9 A/m	Remaining Sections paraded for Gun and Gas Drill.	
"	27/6/17	6.46 A/m	2 Sub-sections paraded and moved off to Training Ground and practiced attack with Battalion.	
		8.0 A/m	Remaining sections under their Section Officers.	
"	28-6-17	8.30 A/m	Company paraded for inspection of Box Respirators & P.H. Helmet by Bde. Gas N.C.O.	
		10.0 A/m	2 sections paraded for a route march.	
"	29-6-17	8 A/m	Company paraded in Field Service Marching Order for a route march. 2nd Lieut. J.B. de Sales, Irish Guards and Lieut. F.B. Wynne-Williams W.Gds. joined Company.	
"	30-6-17	7.30 A/m	2 sub-sections paraded and proceeded to Training Ground for practice attack with Battalion.	
		8.30 A/m	Remaining sub-sections paraded at 8.30 A/m for indirect fire practice and a route march.	

J.H.(?) Captain
Comm'dg. Machine Gun Coy.
3rd Guards Brigade

Army Form C. 2118

WAR DIARY
INTELLIGENCE SUMMARY
(Erase heading not required.)

For Month of July 1917

Vol 20

Instructions regarding War Diaries and Intelligence Summaries are contained in F.S. Regs., Part II. and the Staff Manual respectively. Title Pages will be prepared in manuscript.

3rd Guards Brigade Machine Gun Coy.

Place	Date	Hour	Summary of Events and Information	Remarks and references to Appendices
HOUTKERQUE	1-7-17	8.30 AM	Kit Inspection for Company in billets near HOUTKERQUE.	
"	"	9.30 AM	Divine Service for Presbyterians and Nonconformists.	
"	"	10.15 AM	" " " Church of England.	
"	"	10.0 AM	Billeting party moved off to Divisional Reserve Area to take over billets from 2nd Gds. Bde. M. Gun Coy.	
"	2-7-17	8.15 PM	Company (less Transport) paraded in fighting order and moved off to billets in Gds. Divisional Reserve Area, COPPERNOLLEHOEK (HAZEBROUCK Sht.5a. 12.J.0+60) Route via HOUTKERQUE – WATOU – ST JAN TER BIEZEN – SWITCH ROAD – PESELHOEK.	
PESELHOEK	"	11.0 PM	Company halted for dinner just S.W. of PESELHOEK (Sht 28 N.W. A.26.a)	
"	"	3.0 PM	" paraded and moved off.	
COPPERNOLLEHOEK	"	5.0 PM	" arrived in new billets. Q.M. Stores and Kit moved by lorries. Transport remained at old billets HOUTKERQUE. Horses affected with "Stomatitis" and consequently isolated. Transport of 2nd Gds. Bde. M. Gun Coy. attached temporarily to Company. Party of 3 in billets remained in Bivouacs.	
"	3-7-17	10.0 AM	Company paraded for rifle inspection, camp improvements and digging trench slits for shells in case of hostile shelling.	
"	"	10.0 PM	Working party of 50 other ranks reported to O/c "Q"Special Coy. R.E. at Rail Junction 28/B.10.d.3.4. Nature of work: Relieving trucks to BOESINGHE.	
"	4-7-17	6.0 AM	Working party of 30 Other ranks reported to 183rd Tunnelling Coy. R.E. at junction of HUNTER ST and "X" Lane 28/B.11.d.6.3. Nature of work: Constructing dug-outs.	
"	"	6.0 PM	do	
"	"	11.0 PM	Working party of 60 Other ranks reported to 183rd Tunnelling Coy. R.E. Dump ELVERDINGHE. Nature of work: Carrying material for constructing dug-outs at 28/B.11.d.6.3.	
"	5-7-17	6.0 AM	Working party of 30 other ranks	do
"	"	6.0 PM	do	do
"	"	11.0 PM	do	do
"	6-7-17	6.0 AM	do	do
"	"	6.0 PM	do	do
"	7-7-17	6.0 AM	do	do
"	"	6.0 PM	do	do
"	8-7-17	9.0 AM	2/Lieut. W. J. D. Wightwick, Welsh Guards joined Company. Company paraded in Drill Order, for Gas and Arm Drill.	
"	"	10.30 AM	Lecture to Company by G.O.C. "Machine Guns in the Attack"	
"	9-7-17	6.0 AM	Working party of 30 other ranks reported to 183rd Tunnelling Coy R.E. at 28/B.11.d.6.3. Nature of work: Constructing dug-outs.	

WAR DIARY / INTELLIGENCE SUMMARY

Army Form C. 2118

For month of July 1917 (Contd)

Instructions regarding War Diaries and Intelligence Summaries are contained in F. S. Regs., Part II. and the Staff Manual respectively. Title Pages will be prepared in manuscript.

(Erase heading not required.)

Place	Date	Hour	Summary of Events and Information	Remarks and references to Appendices
FOREST CAMP	17-7-17	10 A	Details paraded for rifle inspection. Box Respirator Drill and Gun Drill	
BOESINGHE	"	11.5 P	Usual indirect fire carried out by indirect fire group till 3 A.m	
FOREST CAMP	18-7-17	10.0 A	Details in Camp paraded for rifle inspection, Box Respirator and Gun Drill	
BOESINGHE	"	11 0 P	Usual indirect fire carried out by indirect fire group till 3 A.m 19-7-17.	
FOREST CAMP	19-7-17	10 0 A	Details in Camp paraded for rifle inspection and Box Respirator Drill, also Gun Drill at 11 A.m	
BOESINGHE	"	11 0 P	Usual indirect fire carried out by indirect fire group till 3 A.m 20-7-17	
FOREST CAMP	20-7-17	10.0 A	Details in Camp paraded for rifle inspection, Box Respirator Drill and Gun Drill at 11 A.m	
BOESINGHE	"	11 0 P	Indirect fire group carried out usual indirect fire till 3 A.m 21-7-17	
"	21-7-17	3.0 A	1st Grenadier Guards and Welsh Guards sections relieved the 2 sections in the line.	
"	"	6 A	Relief complete.	
FOREST CAMP	"	10 0A	Camp Details paraded for rifle inspection	
FOREST ROADS	"	11 30 P	Indirect fire group carried out usual indirect fire till 3 A.m 22-7-17.	
FOREST CAMP	22-7-17	10 0 A	Camp details paraded for rifle inspection, Box Respirator Drill & Gun Drill at 11 A.m	
"	"	11 0 P	Usual indirect fire carried out by indirect fire group till 3 A.m 23-7-17	
"	23-7-17	—	6 O.R. wounded (gas) and 1 Lady Artillery Officer wounded	
FOREST CAMP	"	10 0 A	Camp details paraded for rifle inspection and Box Respirator Drill, Gun Drill at 11 A	
BOESINGHE	"	11 0 P	Indirect fire group carried out usual indirect fire till 3 A.m 24-7-17	
FOREST CAMP	24-7-17	10 0 A	Camp details paraded for rifle inspection, Box Respirator Drill and Gun Drill	
BOESINGHE	"	11 0 P	2 L/G de tails carried out gas in the line	
"	25-7-17	3 A		
"	"	12 N	H.M. Grenadiers and Scots Guards Sections relieved the 2 sections in the line.	
"	"	3 P	Relief complete.	
FOREST CAMP	"	10 0 A	Camp details paraded for rifle inspection and Box Respirator Drill; also Gun Drill at 11 A.m	
BOESINGHE	"	11 0 P	Indirect fire group fired as usual till 3 A.m on 26-7-17	
"	26-7-17	—	(1) A Salisbury – Gen. Cochstream Guards joined Company.	
FOREST CAMP	"	10 0 A	Camp details paraded for rifle inspection, Box Respirator drill and Gun drill at 11 A.m	
BOESINGHE	"	11 0 P	Indirect fire group fired as usual till 3 A.m 27-7-17	
FOREST CAMP	27-7-17	3.45 P	Relief of the line started and moved off equipped for attack.	
BOESINGHE	"	6 0 A	Relief complete.	
FOREST CAMP	"	—	Enemy aircraft dropped bombs on aircraft during the night on camp causing 8 casualties in the Coy	
			viz. 2 Sgts killed, 1 Sgt wounded, 2 L/Cpls wounded, and 6 wounded O.R.	
BOESINGHE	"	5.0 P	The 3rd Battalion Coldstream Guards, whose front line extended from left to right – front line finished an outpost line on the line BABOON SUPPORT, DONTEUSE HOUSE – S.W. corner ARTILLERY WOOD – Corner. Post Cobalt C7a49. (Sht 20 SW4 (French Map)) to the BIXSCHOETE)	J.B.C. & A. A.D.S.S./Forms/C.2118.

WAR DIARY

INTELLIGENCE SUMMARY

For month of July 1917 (Contd).

Army Form C. 2118

Place	Date	Hour	Summary of Events and Information	Remarks and references to Appendices
BOESINGHE	27-7-17	5.0 A M	There was no enemy of aeroplanes reporting no enemy infantry West of STEENBEEK - The 2nd Battalion succeeded in establishing outpost line as follows B.11.b.3.9. - Southern edge of ARTILLERY WOOD - POND at B.6.b. central - BOIS FARM - B.6.a.8.8. and got in touch with 113th Inf. Bde. on right and 3rd trench on left. 1 sub. section (3 machine guns) under Lt. A.F. PURVIS of this Company moved forward with front line across Canal to assist in the consolidation of the above outpost line. Guns were put in following positions. Right gun at B6.a.9.5. and Left gun at B.6.a.8.9. Another machine gun and team was moved up to position at B.6.b. Central near BOIS FARM thus making 3 Guns on the most front line. It was discovered that enemy had no movements	
"	28-7-17	—	his trench system West of STEENBEEK as reported by aircraft.	
FOREST CAMP	"	10 A.M.	Camp details paraded for Rifle & inspection, Box Respirator Drill and Gun Drill at M.G.	
BOESINGHE	29-7-17	0 A.M.	1 sub-section (3 M.Guns) under 2nd Lt. A.H. WILSON and 1 sub section (3 guns) under 2nd Lt. PRINCE GEORGE relieved the remaining 2 in fighting order to relieve the following guns in the line. 3 guns in outpost line to sections of 2nd Lt. A.H. WILSON with 1 gun from 2nd Lt. PRINCE GEORGE's section. The remaining gun and team of PRINCE GEORGE's relieved a gun in the tank line. Rest complete at M.G.	
"	"		2/Lt. PRINCE GEORGE slightly wounded - Sergt J. WILL took charge of sub section initially.	
"	30-7-17	4 A.M.	4 Gun teams from 1st Grenadiers and Welsh Guards Section paraded in fighting order for attack under D/Sergt MA NYNGHE and relieved Lt. F.R. WYNNE WILLIAMS at GOULDY FARM.	
"	"	6 A.M.	Lt. E.N. HAGUE & Lt. NORRY and their Sections moved into position with the section under 2nd Lt. A.H. WILSON move to operate in accordance with the Divisional Machine Gun Officer's orders.	
"	"	8 A.M.	Barrage of fire during forthcoming attack on 31st.	
"	"		2nd sub-section of 2nd Lt. PRINCE GEORGE's Grenadiers Gun of 2nd Bn. Grenadier Guards, 2/Lt. D.E. SMITH moved off E6. The two to take part in the attack on zero day (31st) jointly. 2/Lt. D.E. SMITH sub-section of 2nd Co. Bn. Grenadier Guards. 2nd Lt. A.F. PURVIS to take part in the attack on 31st to move off for the same as well. 2/Lt. A.F. PURVIS Lieut. 50 O.R. (Forward from transport details).	
"	"	"	2/Lt. R. NEEDHAM in exchange of 2/Lt. J. KERR moved No.8 Gun (by 31) moved M.G.800 rounds. S.A.S. from WHITE HOPE CORNER to STEAM MILL Dump.	
"	"	11 o AM	2/Lt. R. NEEDHAM moved from EVERDINGHE CHATEAU to B.11.d.6.3. same place as Bn. H.Q. 2/Lt. A.W. NELSON to 2nd sub-section attached to 1st Bn. Welsh Guards for the attack. The place was taken up by 2/Lt. fil. A. BURNS.	
"	31-7-17	Zero hour 3.50 AM	The XIV Corps attacked the enemy in conjunction with 2nd Guards Brigade on right and left. 3 Eden 38th Division attacked on right of Guards Division and 1st French Division (201st Regt)	

1875 Wt. W593/826 1,000,000 4/15 J.B.C. & A. A.D.S.S./Forms/C.2118.

WAR DIARY
INTELLIGENCE SUMMARY

Army Form C. 2118

For month of July (contd.)

Place	Date	Hour	Summary of Events and Information	Remarks and references to Appendices
SINGHE	31-7-17	Zero hour 3.50 A.M.	on left. The b[attalio]ns of this company were grouped as follows: 1 sub-section Scots Gds under Lt. H.C.A. Bundy East of ditch supporting advance of Welsh Guards (100 Rs) to 1st and 2nd objectives on left of Brigade front. 1 sub-section of 4th Bn Grenadier Guards supporting advance of 1st Bn. Grenadiers Guards on right to 1st and 2nd objectives under Lt. J.S.G. Free. 1 sub-section of Scots Guards under Lt. A.F. Burns supporting advance of 2nd Bn Scots Guards. 1 sub-section of 4 Grenadiers Guards with the 4th Br Grenadier Guards under Lt. D.E. Smith. The 1st Grenadier Guards section under Lt. N. Wayne being in direct barrage from zero plus 30 to zero plus 154, when it cleared to Coy H.Q. position tin garage B.5.c.9.1. 3 guns of Nelson Guards section under Lt. M.A. Hughes were in position about GOUY FARM, advancing later to position about SANKE'S FARM V.25.c.6.3. 1 gun in reserve near Company H.Q. Lt. F.B. Wayne with one section (Pve Gebreschi Ry wounded) Lt. A.G. Labalmondière Jones told off to salvage of belt boxes etc of barrage groups. Lt. A.G. Labalmondière Jones without a hitch and about zero plus 130 the BLACK LINE was taken. H.C.M.A.F. Burns established M.G. Strong Point on left flank of BLUE and BLACK LINES about U.25.c.08 and U.25.a.5.4 and at once reported his position to Coy H.Q. Lt. J.S.G. Free in charge of 4th Gren Gds sub-section (Pve Gebreschi Ry wounded) also established his guns about C.1.a.4.3. Lt. A.F. Burns had 1 or killed & 3 wounded while holding the line. Serge Hill had no casualties. At Zero plus 304 the advance continued to the GREEN LINE, this was also taken without a hitch. Lt. A.F. Burns consolidated with 2 machine Guns on left flank about U.20.c.6.9 Gunning trench and at U.20.c.7.8. Lt. A.F. Burns was severely wounded and Serge J.G. Newlove took charge. Lt. D.E. Smith consolidated M.G. Positions at CAPTAIN'S FARM U.26.d.15.7 and at FOURCHE FARM U.26.d.15.3. During advance from BLACK to GREEN LINE, Lt. F.B. Wayne Williamson forward with 2 Machine Guns to WOOD 15 and as soon as the GREEN LINE was secured advanced to S.E. corner of WOOD 15 with 1 Coy of 3rd Coy J.B.C. The GREEN LINE positions were then visited and if the German reverse at WOOD 15 thought forward and placed near MAJOR'S FARM.	

WAR DIARY or INTELLIGENCE SUMMARY

Army Form C. 2118

For month of July 1917 (Contd).

Place	Date	Hour	Summary of Events and Information	Remarks and references to Appendices
BOESINGHE	31.7.17	2.50 a.m. Zero Hour	It was decided not to move forward more guns as 18 guns in direct barrage group had moved forward until D.M.G.O. and staff of 4 Guards Bde could ascertain about SAVILE'S FARM, ABRI WOOD and WOOD FARM HOUSE. Lieut. Neilson wounded during afternoon until 2/Lt R. Wylie to take charge. LIEUT. R. Henderson in charge of fatigue party of 50 O.R. from Transport Lines of Guards M. Gun Companies moved 50,000 rounds S.A.A. from STEAM MILL to ABRI WOOD (Central D.M.G.O.'s Dump). 2 guns remained throughout near Brigade H.Q. under Sergt. Gilson of 3 replenishing from 3rd Echelon barrage at Zero plus 15th. Left wing 3rd Echelon barrage 1st Guards Bde M.G.Coy. All guns were Company relieved following night by 1st Guards Bde M.G.Coy. All guns were out of the line by 12 midnight. Total casualties of the Company were not heavy during the attack as holding the line afterwards but they were heavy before the attack as the Company was in the line for 18 days before Zero day. Total casualties: 1 Officer killed, 3 Officers wounded, 7 O.Ranks killed, 36 O.Ranks wounded.	

M.J.P. Captain,
Commdg 3 M.Gun Coy.
3rd Gds. Bde.

WAR DIARY of 3rd Guards Brigade M. Gun Coy.

Army Form C. 2118

INTELLIGENCE SUMMARY

for month of August 1917

(Erase heading not required.)

Instructions regarding War Diaries and Intelligence Summaries are contained in F. S. Regs., Part II. and the Staff Manual respectively. Title Pages will be prepared in manuscript.

Place	Date	Hour	Summary of Events and Information	Remarks and references to Appendices
FOREST CAMP	1-8-17	10.0 A	Coy paraded for rifle and Box respirator inspection and overhauling of equipment	
— do —	2-8-17	10.0 A	Coy paraded for rifle inspection and Box respirator drill	
— do —	3-8-17	9.30 A	Coy paraded for rifle inspection and Box Respirator drill	
— do —	4-8-17	10.0 A	Coy paraded for rifle inspection and Company drill	
— do —	"	2.30 P	1st Grenadier Guards and 1st Welsh Guards Sections paraded and moved off for the line	
BOESINGHE			Sectn. 1st Welsh Guards had 4 guns in front line and 1st Grenadier Guards 4 guns in support	
— do —	5-8-17	10 A	Remainder of Company paraded for rifle inspection, Box Respirator and Physical Drill	
— do —	6-8-17	9 A	Remainder of Company paraded for N.F.A instruction and Gas Drill	
BOESINGHE	7-8-17	1 A	Relief of 8 Guns in the line completed by 86th M.G. Coy. M.Gun Corps	
FOREST CAMP	"	6.15 A	Company paraded and marched off by march route to PLAISTOW CAMP at F.9.a.39 (late 3) Belgium and France (4000) PROVEN AREA.	
PLAISTOW CAMP	"	11.30 A	Company under 2 i/c Capt. and accommodated in E. S. L. Tents	
— do —	8-8-17	7.0 A	Company paraded at 7.0 AM and left for Box Respirator Drill, Lewis Gun washing	
— do —	9-8-17	9.0 A	all gun kit and equipment. 3 NCO's + Pts 7 Guards Coy joined Company	
— do —			Company paraded and inspected: for Box Respirators inspection, Arm drill and Elementary gas.	
— do —	10-8-17	4.0 A	The 3rd Bttn Gren'r Gds Section found two guns for anti-aircraft work at PROVEN DUMP	
— do —		7.0 A	Remainder paraded at 7.0 AM and left for Box Respirator Drill, Lewis gun washing	
— do —		9.0 A	and aeroplane Elementary Gas	
— do —		4.0 P	The 2nd Grenadier Guards Section found two gun teams for anti-aircraft work at PROVEN DUMP	
— do —	11-8-17	9.0 A	Company paraded for Arm drill and route march. Elementary Gas	
— do —		4.0 P	1st & 4th Grenadier Guards Section relieved the two guns of 3rd Grenadier Guards at PROVEN DUMP	
— do —	12-8-17	7.15 A	Company paraded for Divine Service. 2Lt L.F. Balson, Welsh Guards, joined Company	
— do —			as N.C.O. and	
— do —	13-8-17		Company paraded for inspection of Box Respirator and P.H. Helmets by Brigade Gas N.C.O. and	
— do —		3.30 P	2nd Bttn Gds Section arm drill and inspection of belts and belt boxes	

1875. Wt. W593/826 1,000,000 4/15 J.B.C. & A. A.D.S.S./Forms/C. 2118.

WAR DIARY of 3rd Guards Brigade M. Gun Coy. Army Form C. 2118
INTELLIGENCE SUMMARY
For month of August 1917.
(Continued).

(Erase heading not required.)

Instructions regarding War Diaries and Intelligence Summaries are contained in F. S. Regs., Part II. and the Staff Manual respectively. Title Pages will be prepared in manuscript.

2

Place	Date	Hour	Summary of Events and Information	Remarks and references to Appendices
PLAISTOW CAMP	13-8-17	4 P.M.	The 2nd Lieut G.A. Lockwood returned for anti-aircraft gun team of 1st Gren. Gds. at PROVEN DUMP	
— do —	14-8-17	8 A.M.	The Company paraded at the usual hour for gun drill, arm drill and gun drill without use of Compass Tang.	
		5 P.M.	Captain Mr. Hockin left Company to take Command of 2nd Guards Bgde Company at BEAN MTN GUN Company.	
— do —	15-8-17	L. O P.	Two anti-aircraft gun teams of 2nd Guards Bgde engaged with drawn from PROVEN DUMP.	
		8.30 A	The Coy paraded for the following training: Physical Training, Arm Drill, Lecture by Dunbar Officer, Gun Drill, Mechanism and Semaphore.	
— do —	16-8-17	6.30 A	The Company paraded for the following training: Gun Drill, Stoppages, Coy. Gas Mask reading, Semaphore, Testing messages, Stripping and cleaning Gun and use of Clinometer.	
— do —	17-8-17	6.30 A	The Company paraded for the following training: Physical training, Arm Drill, Gas Drill, Gun Drill, Mechanism, etc. and cleaning of guns.	
— do —	18-8-17	6.30 A	The Coy paraded for following training: Physical Drill Sematcsh Action Control and	
		9.0 P.M.	Flag reading and Gun Drill. 9/Pte W/ 2 D. Brighcock Field Ambulance, admitted to Hospital.	
— do —	19-8-17	9.15 A	Inspection of all gun and personal kit.	
		10.15	The company paraded for Divine Service.	
— do —	20-8-17	5.30 A	The Coy paraded for the following training: Physical training, Semaphore and Map reading. Arm Drill, Gas Drill, Care and cleaning of guns, Bombs, before during and after firing.	
— do —	21-8-17	9 P.A.	The Coy paraded for the following training: Arm Drill, & Lectures Gas Drill. Gas & 5.30 and 10 A.M. & 3rd Section sat practice	
— do —	22-8-17	8.30 A.	The Coy paraded for the following training: Physical Training, Stripping, Care and cleaning of guns and Bombs. B. D. and A firing. Indication & Recognition of targets.	
— do —	23-8-17	6.0 A	The Coy paraded for the following training: Physical training, Lecture on First Ord man, Cov for all NCOs and No 1s. Indication and Recognition of Targets. Indirect fire practice for 2 Lecture, Signaller employed or manual.	
— do —	24-8-17	6.30 A	The Coy paraded for following training: Gun Drill, Arm Drill and Practice. Semaphore – 2 Lectures on Indirect fire practice. & lectures on Indication and Recognition of Targets.	
— do —	25-8-17	8.30 A	The Coy paraded for Company Drill and Practice on use of anti-aircraft sights.	
		11 P.	The Coy paraded and moved off to attend Ceremony for Presentation of French Decorations to the Guards Division by General Anthoine commanding 1st French Army. Place of Assembly ground at F.28, L.B.29 Belgium + France (HUSSEL).	

1875 Wt. W593/826 1,000,000 4/15 J.B.C. & A. A.D.S.S./Forms/C. 2118.

Army Form C. 2118

WAR DIARY of 3rd Gds. Bde. M. Gun Coy.

INTELLIGENCE SUMMARY

For month of August 1917 (Continued)

No. 3

Instructions regarding War Diaries and Intelligence Summaries are contained in F.S. Regs., Part II. and the Staff Manual respectively. Title Pages will be prepared in manuscript.

(Erase heading not required.)

Place	Date	Hour	Summary of Events and Information	Remarks and references to Appendices
PLAISIR CAMP	26-8-17	9.45 am	The Company paraded and moved off to camp at BALLANTINE FOREST. (A 10.d. 9.7) Shut 28 (1/40,000)	
BALLANTINE FOREST	"	12 noon	Company arrived in Camp.	
"	27-8-17	10.30 am	Section paraded and checked gun kit preparatory to going into the line.	
"	"	11.30 am	The 1st Grenadier Guards, 4th Grenadier Guards and Welsh Guards Sections finished 4 Guns each paraded and moved off to relieve 58th & 87th M. Gun Company, Machine Gun Corps in the line.	
LANGEMARCK	"	—	Disposition of Guns as follows:—	
			1st Grenadier Gds. Section. MONTMIRAIL FARM Group. 4 Guns { 1 A.A. Gun at Section H.Q. / 1 gun at U.15.c.5.4 / 1 " at U.15.c.5.5 / 1 " at U.15.d.3.8 }	
			4th Grenadier Gds. Section. STATION Group. 4 Guns { 1 gun at U.21.c.5.5 / 1 " U.21.c.9.4.5 / 1 " U.21.d.4.9 / 1 " U.21.d.5.5½ }	All 20.S.N14 BIXSCHOOTE 1/10,000
			1st Welsh Guards Section. JAPAN HOUSE Group. 4 Guns { 1 gun at U.23.a.5.5 / 1 " U.16.d.7½.2 / 1 " U.16.c.6.4½ / 1 " U.16.c.5.4½ }	
			Company Headquarters at PINSON FARM.	
BALLANTINE FOREST	28-8-17	2 pm	R.Coy. Company Parade.	
"	"	10 am	Remainder of Company paraded for rifle and box-respirator inspection. 1 O.R. Killed viz: 3/8 2714 Stewart, Grenadier Gds. joined Company 29/5/17	
"	29-8-17	L.30 pm	The 2nd G.G. and 3rd G.G. Sections paraded and moved off to the line finding 4 Guns for A.A. defence at T.6.R. in position near ASKI WOOD. (BIXSCHOOTE Sheet 1/10,000)	
"	"	2.30 pm	Remainder of Company paraded for rifle inspection.	
"	30-8-17	9 am	" " " "	
"	"	2 pm	" " " "	
"	"	3.30 pm	Welsh Guards team paraded and moved off to relieve JAPAN HOUSE Group.	
LANGEMARCK	"	6 pm	Relief Complete. Casualties: 3 O.R.s wounded. 2 " killed 2 tanks knocked out	
BALLANTINE FOREST	31-8-17	9 am	Remainder of Company in Camp paraded for rifle inspection.	
"	"	2 pm	Welsh Guard team paraded and moved off to relieve the remaining Group in the line.	
LANGEMARCK	"	6 pm	Relief Comp'd G.E.	

1875 Wt. W593/826 1,000,000 4/15 J.B.C. & A. A.D.S.S./Forms/C.2118.

WAR DIARY of 3rd Gds Bde M.Gun Coy. Army Form C. 2118
or
INTELLIGENCE SUMMARY for month of August 1917
(Continued)
(Erase heading not required.)

The following Honours & Awards have been granted to the Officer & N.C.O.s of this Coy enumerated below, during the month of August.

Captain T.A. Taft, Coldstream Guards — MILITARY CROSS
Lieut. E.N. Hague, Grenadier Guards — MILITARY CROSS
Lieut. A.T. Purvis, Scots Guards — MILITARY CROSS
Lieut. T.B. Wynne-Williams, Welsh Guards — MILITARY CROSS
No.1302 Sgt. E. Byng, Machine Gun Guards — MILITARY MEDAL
No.755 L/Cpl. A.J. Burns, Machine Gun Guards — MILITARY MEDAL

C.P. Hague Lieut
for Captain
Comdg 3rd M.Gun Coy.
3rd Guards Brigade.

App: 31.

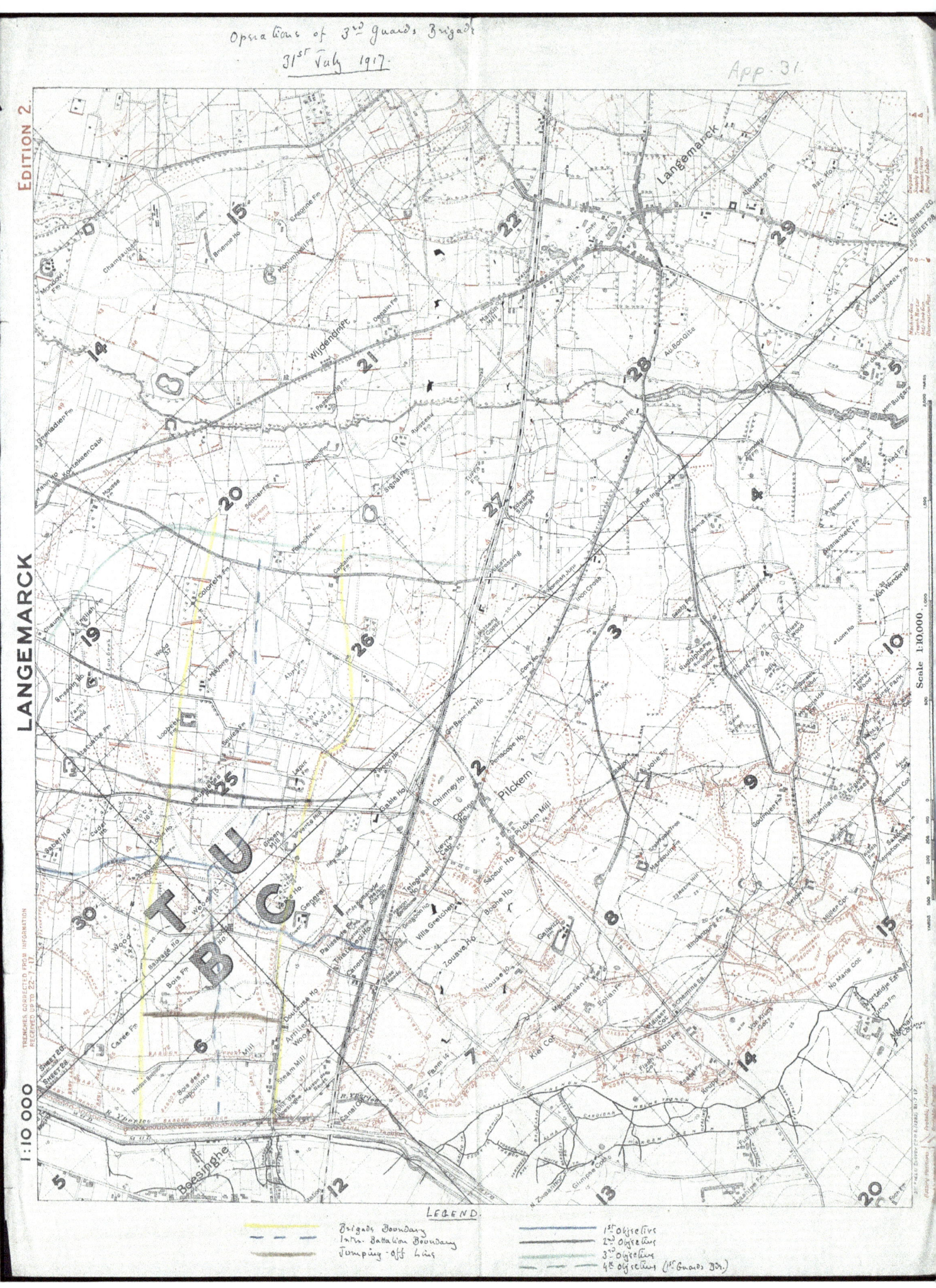

WAR DIARY

INTELLIGENCE SUMMARY

(Erase heading not required.)

Army Form C. 2118

For Month of September, 1917

Instructions regarding War Diaries and Intelligence Summaries are contained in F.S. Regs., Part II. and the Staff Manual respectively. Title Pages will be prepared in manuscript.

3rd Guards Brigade Machine Gun Company

Place	Date	Hour	Summary of Events and Information	Remarks and references to Appendices
FOREST CAMP	1-9-17	9.30 A	Remainder of Company in Camp paraded for rifle inspection.	
LANGEMARCK	"	-	Sections in the line had 1 other rank wounded.	
FOREST CAMP	2-9-17	9.30 A	Remainder of Company in Camp paraded for rifle and Box Respirator inspection.	
LANGEMARCK	"	-	Sections in the line had 3 other ranks killed in action and 1 other rank wounded slightly at duty.	
FOREST CAMP	3-9-17	9.30 A	Remainder of Company in Camp paraded for rifle and Box Respirator inspection.	
"	4-9-17	"	" " " " " "	
"	5-9-17	"	" " " " " "	
LANGEMARCK	"	11.30 A	Relief complete. Teams on the line relieved by 1st Gds Bde M. Gun Company.	
FOREST CAMP	6-9-17	9.30 A	Company less Sections returning from the line paraded for Kit, rifle, revolver inspection.	
"	7-9-17	"	Company paraded for arms & Box respirators drill, stripping and cleaning of M. Guns.	
"	8-9-17	8.0 A	Company paraded by Sections for Baths at DECOUCK FARM.	
"	9-9-17	8.30 A	Company paraded for Divine Service.	
"	10-9-17	9.30 A	Company paraded for Camp fatigue.	
"	"	1.0 P	Working party of 40 other ranks reported to R.E. ONDANK DUMP for screening (4 hours).	
"	11-9-17	9.30 A	Company paraded for 1 hour's training under Section Officers followed by Camp improvements.	
"	12-9-17	9.30 A	Company paraded for baths by Sections at DECOUCK FARM.	
"	"	12.45 P	Working party of 50 other ranks reported to R.E. ONDANK DUMP for screening (4 hours). 1 O.R. severely wounded by aircraft bomb.	
"	13-9-17	9 A.M.	Company paraded for packing guns, kit on limbers ready for moving to WELLINGTON CAMP. (29/B.G.d.I.S.)	
"	"	6.45 P	Company handed over and moved off. Fighting limbers accompanied Sections. Remainder of transport and Q.M. Stores remaining in FOREST CAMP.	
WELLINGTON CAMP	14-9-17	8.0 A	Company paraded. Occupying tented and hutted lines and Bivouacs.	
"	"	9.0 A	Company paraded for rifle inspection and Camp fatigue. Working party of 50 O.R.	
"	15-9-17	6.30 A	reported to Divisional Salvage Company for fatigue.	
"	"	9.0 A	Working party of 50 O.R. reported to Divl. Salvage Company for fatigue.	
"	"	-	Remainder of Coy. paraded for rifle, box respirator inspection followed by Camp improvements.	

WAR DIARY

INTELLIGENCE SUMMARY

(Erase heading not required.)

Army Form C. 2118

For month of September 1917
(Continued)

Instructions regarding War Diaries and Intelligence Summaries are contained in F.S. Regs., Part II. and the Staff Manual respectively. Title Pages will be prepared in manuscript.

Place	Date	Hour	Summary of Events and Information	Remarks and references to Appendices
WELLINGTON CAMP	15-9-17	—	2/Lt J.H.Hillik, Coldstream Guards and 2/Lt A.G.J. de Vomes, Grenadier Guards joined Company.	
"	16-9-17	4.30 A.M.	Working party of 25 O.R. reported at RUGBY DUMP for fatigue.	
"	"	5.30 P.M.	" " " " " " " "	
"	17-9-17	4.30 A.M.	" " " " " " " "	
"	"	5.30 P.M.	" " " " " " " "	
"	"	9.0 A.M.	Remainder of Company paraded by Sections for Arms drill, gas drill and Camp fatigue.	
"	"	2.45 P.M.	Company paraded by Sections for Baths at DECOUCK FARM.	
"	18-9-17	5.0 A.M.	Working party of 75 O.R. reported at RUGBY DUMP for fatigue.	
"	"	5.30 P.M.	" " " " " " " "	
"	"	9.0 A.M.	Remainder of Company paraded by Sections for Box Respirator and rifle inspection, Physical Training and Camp Fatigues.	
"	19-9-17	9.0 A.M.	Company paraded for inspection of arms and Box Respirators followed by Camp fatigue. Brigadier General inspected Camp.	
"	20-9-17	12 noon	Company paraded and moved off to entrain at ELVERDINGHE STATION to move to POINT CAMP N° PROVEN. 19/N 30.C.2.7.	
POINT CAMP	"	3.30 P.M.	Company detrained at PROVEN STATION and marched to Camp.	
"	21-9-17	9.30 A.M.	Company paraded for training under Section Officers.	
"	"	2.30 P.M.	Company paraded and moved off to new Camp at MAISON BLEUE F.M., HERZEELE.	
HERZEELE	"	4.30 P.M.	Company arrived in Camp.	
"	22-9-17	9.0 A.M.	Company paraded at 9 A.M. for gun drill, stoppages, Immediate Action and Fire Orders.	
"	23-9-17	11.6 A.M.	Company paraded for Divine Service	
"	24-9-17	7.15 A.M.	No.2 and 3 Sections paraded in fighting order and moved off for training with 4th Bn Grenadier Guards and 1st Bn Welsh Guards respectively during the morning.	
"	"	1.0 P.M.	No.1 and 4 Sections paraded for similar training in the afternoon with 1st Bn Grenadier Guards and 2nd Bn Scots Guards respectively.	
"	25-9-17	7.30 A.M.	No.1 and 4 Sections paraded for training with 1 Bn Grenadier Gds and 3rd Bn Scots Gds respectively.	
"	"	"	No.2 and 3 Sections paraded for similar training with 4th Bn Grenadier Guards and 1st Bn Welsh Guard respectively.	
"	26-9-17	9.0 A.M.	Company paraded for inspection of Box Respirators by the Brigade Gas N.C.O. After inspection lectures were delivered to the N.C.Os and Officers.	
"	"	9.0 P.M.	A test patrol from each of No.1 and 3 Sections reported to 2/Bn Welsh Gds respectively for acting with advanced Guards in a Tactical scheme.	

Army Form C. 2118

WAR DIARY
INTELLIGENCE SUMMARY

For month of September 1917 (Continued).

Instructions regarding War Diaries and Intelligence Summaries are contained in F.S. Regs., Part II. and the Staff Manual respectively. Title Pages will be prepared in manuscript.

(Erase heading not required.)

Place	Date	Hour	Summary of Events and Information	Remarks and references to Appendices
HERZEELE	27.9.17	9.0 A.M.	No. 2 Section paraded and moved off reporting to O.C. Hostile Troops at 8 A.M. to take part in Tactical Scheme.	
"	"	8.15 A.M.	Remainder of Company paraded in fighting order and proceeded to GALLOIA and there assembled in Brigade Reserve.	
"	28.9.17	7.30 A.M.	A Subsection from each of No. 1 and 3 Sections paraded and carried out Tactical Scheme with Battalions.	
"	"	7 A.M.	No. 4 Section paraded and moved off reporting to O.C. Hostile Troops at 8 A.M. to take part in the said scheme.	
"	29.9.17	8.30 A.M.	The Company paraded together with transport and marched to PLAISTOW CAMP. Transport proceeded separately arriving in Camp at 11 A.M.	
PLAISTOW CAMP	"	12 noon	Company arrived in Camp.	
"	30.9.17	10.15 A.M.	Company paraded and attended Divine Service.	

W.H.P. Kenyon Captain,
Commdg. M.Gun Coy.,
3rd Guards Brigade.

Army Form C. 2118

WAR DIARY
INTELLIGENCE SUMMARY

For month of October 1917

Vol 23

3rd Guards Brigade Machine Gun Company

Place	Date	Hour	Summary of Events and Information	Remarks and references to Appendices
PLAISTOW CAMP	1-10-17	8.0A	Company paraded by Sections for Range practice on Range at F.4.C. Central (Sht 27 (Belgium France)) 1/40000) at R.E. Schwede; jointh company detached from Irish Guards.	
do	2-10-17	9.0A	Company paraded for Company Drill, fire orders, Indirect fire practice, laying out lines of fire + direction.	
do	3-10-17	9.30A	Sections paraded for Baths at Y.x.36.a.16. (Sht. 19 Belgium France 1/40000). Sections on returning from Baths had instructions on sorting.	
do	4-10-17	9.0A	Company paraded for Company drill, map work and indirect fire practice.	
do			Backwald's Crew firing drill and foot instruction. Lectures Gun Drill, Stripping & cleaning.	
do	5-10-17	9.30A	Company paraded for a lecture by E.O. afterwards performed M Gun training under Section officers.	
do			Methods of classes paraded for instructions, gun drill, stripping and care and cleaning.	
do	6-10-17	9.0A	Company paraded and moved off to PROVEN STATION when entrained for ELVERDINGHE.	
			Company detrained and marched to WELLINGTON CAMP, taking own from 87th M Gun Coy, M Gun Corps.	
ELVERDINGHE		12 noon	Company billeted and Q.M.S. Co. moved to Box Camp by road.	
WELLINGTON CAMP		8.30A	Transport and Q.M.S. Co. moved to Box Camp by road.	
do		2.30P	Company arrived. Accommodation, Tents and Bivouacs.	
		5.0P	Nos 1 and 4 Sections paraded and moved off to relieve 2 Sections of the 87th M.G. Coy in the line. M.11. c.2.3 to V.15. Cont. at Sk.33. B. Carrying parties of 30 men each also paraded with three sections.	
			Carry wanted to Section in Camp paraded for rifle inspection.	
do	7-10-17	6A	2 Sections in line relieved by 2 Sections of 87th M Gun Coy. Relief complete at 10P.	
		10 A	Sections in the line relieved. Casualties 3 O.R. Killed. 1 O.R. wounded.	
		1.30P	Teams from the line arrived.	
do	8-10-17		Company paraded and moved off for the line taking up positions for Machine Gun Barrage.	
		4.45P	Company to Supply the attack by Guards Division on Zero Day.	
BROEMBEEK	9-10-17	5.20A	Zero Day. Guards Division attacked the enemy defences in front of HOUTHULST FOREST in conjunction with 88th Brigade on right and 29th French Regiment on left. Lt. Johnson Gun of the Company were in two groups viz forward Group. 3 Sections under Lt. D.E. Smith. 5 Guns from forward group were at short range on the R.T. barrage, and M.G.M. Group under Lt. D.E. Smith. 5 Guns from forward group were at short range on the line GB to give direct overhead fire from Zero, and strong points on the North side of the BROEMBEEK. R.M.G. Group opened fire at Zero on strong points NEY Fm. and GRUYSELLE FM, lifting at Zero plus 13 mins on to barrage line moving from V.10.c.9.1 V.11.a.1.9. Hill Zero plus 15 mins all then came to 6.0. Terminal group opened O.B.M.S.T. FARM and A.D.S.S./Forms/C. 2118. At Zero plus 3 hrs 3 forms at concentration on SUEZ FARM, LOUVOIS FM.	

WAR DIARY continued

Army Form C. 2118.

Instructions regarding War Diaries and Intelligence Summaries are contained in F. S. Regs., Part II. and the Staff Manual respectively. Title Pages will be prepared in manuscript.

INTELLIGENCE SUMMARY

For month of October, 1917.

(Erase heading not required.)

Place	Date	Hour	Summary of Events and Information	Remarks and references to Appendices
BROENBEEK	9-10-17		Lifted at Zero plus 2 hours 10 minutes on to line running from U.5.c.8.3 to U.5.2.6.7. Coming thro' at Zero plus 3 hours 35 minutes. All objectives were taken. Casualties during this operation 3 O.R. killed and 7 O.R. wounded. 50 belt boxes were destroyed by shell fire at belt filling station.	
WELLINGTON CAMP.	"	8.0 P.M.	Carrying party of 30 O.R. paraded under Lt. K.E. Schwedes to assist in carrying out guns etc. of the operation.	
— do —	"	12 noon	Detail paraded and moved to BURKE CAMP.	
BURKE CAMP	"	3.0 P.M.	Company arrived from the line.	
— do —	10-10-17	10.30 A.M.	Company paraded for Gun Kit inspection. Lt K.E. Schwedes with a party of 20 men paraded at 7.30 P.M. and proceeded to CRAONNE FARM and relieved all belt boxes and guns not that had been left behind.	
			Lt. E.N. Hague. M.C. 2nd in Command transferred to England for 6 months light duty.	
— do —	11-10-17	—	Company relieved the 2nd Guards Brigade M.Gun Coy in the line and moved off as under:-	
		1.30 P.M.	Sub sections found by No's 3 and 4 sections	
		5.0 P.M.	No's 1 and 3 sections and company headquarters. Guns were found for the left sector of the new line as follows:-	
			8 guns in the front and support line divided into two groups. Left section H.Q. at LOUVOIS FARM and the right section H.Q. near SUEZ FARM. 4 guns at Cemetery, NEY WOOD for S.O.S. barrage. 2 guns in reserve at CRAONNE FARM.	
			Bn. H.Qrs at MONTMIRAIL FARM.	
BROENBEEK	13-10-17	5.0 A.M.	Bde H.Qrs. TA to M.G.N.C and 2/KR.2-N. Stewart were wounded while the relief was in progress by a shell. The same shell caused casualties among N team of the right section and knocked out a gun which was replaced by one from the barrage gun. 2/Lieut F.L.T Barlow took over command of the left T.A. till 2/Lt. got wounded. The Command of the company was later taken over by Captain 2/Abel Smith. M.C. of 1st Gds Bde M. Gun Coy. Relief completed.	
			On arriving the left sector, Lt Barlow found that the Held Guard had already established the machine gun Posts objective for the following day, and 1 M.Gun was in the front line in a FAIDHERBE X Roads covering the road running North.	

Army Form C. 2118

WAR DIARY *continued*

INTELLIGENCE SUMMARY for month of October 1917

Instructions regarding War Diaries and Intelligence Summaries are contained in F.S. Regs., Part II. and the Staff Manual respectively. Title Pages will be prepared in manuscript.

Place	Date	Hour	Summary of Events and Information	Remarks and references to Appendices
BROEMBEEK	12-10-17	—	Two guns near STRONG POINT covering our junction with the FRENCH on the left — one gun in reserve at LOUVOIS FARM. The 2 Bn Grenadier Guards having established objective on the night. At Barlow reconnoitred a position for a M Gun in the new line about U.6.C.3.6.b. A support gun from SUEZ FARM taking the place of the one installed at the new position. 2 Lt G Wyne-Williams M.C. held G2 and 2/Lt Howorth-Tomson Gn wounded (Gas) During the night Ney Wood was heavily shelled causing some casualties, gassed.	
— do —	13/10/17	—	Guns remained in same positions. No counter attack developed. An internal relief was carried out. The teams in reserve at NEY WOOD relieving the front line. During night the NEY WOOD guns employed indirect harassing fire on the neighbourhood of COLOMBO HOUSE. During 2/Lt G. Smith Grenadier Guards wounded (Gas).	
— do —	13/10/17	—	During the night the front line guns were fired direct on the German front line and communications.	
— do —	14/15/10/17	—	Company relieved by 2nd Gds. de M. Gun Coy and returned to BURKE CAMP. Relief was complete after Ye. Total Casualties during this tour in the line:— 2 Officers wounded by Arty fire; 3 Officers wounded (Gas); 3 O.R. killed by Hely fire; 17 O.R. wounded and 7 O.R. wounded Gas (Gas).	
BURKE CAMP	"	12 noon	Company arrived from the line.	
— do —	15/10/17	10 A	Company paraded in clean fatigue dress for a roll call by section.	
— do —	16/10/17	9.30 A	Company paraded at 9.30 A.M. under Section arrangements for inspection of rifles and gas appliances.	
— do —	17/10/17	8.55A	Company paraded in marching order and moved off to ONDANK where it entrained. On arriving at PROVEN it detrained and marched to billets at PEGWELL CAMP 27/E.5.d.6.1. Q.M. Stores and Kit was moved by lorry.	
PEGWELL CAMP	"	11.30 A	Company arrived. Transport moved by road with all the Brigade transport. Route. INTERNATIONAL CORNER — COUTHOVE CHATEAU.	
— do —	18/10/17	9.0 A	Coys paraded for Drill, cleaning and inspection of gunkit and cleaning up Camp.	
— do —	19/10/17	8.30 A	Company paraded for Drill, MGun training and Kit inspection.	
— do —	"	9.50 A	Part of Transport paraded and moved off to WATTEN Area, spending night 19/20 at ZERMEZEELE.	
— do —	20/10/17	10.15 A	Leading Party of 10 men and Transport E paraded and moved off to PROVEN STATION	

19/20. Wt. W593/826 1,000,000 4/15 J.B.C. & A. A.D.S.S./Forms/C.2118.

Army Form C. 2118.

WAR DIARY *continued*
INTELLIGENCE SUMMARY

For month of October 1917

Instructions regarding War Diaries and Intelligence Summaries are contained in F. S. Regs., Part II. and the Staff Manual respectively. Title Pages will be prepared in manuscript.

Place	Date	Hour	Summary of Events and Information	Remarks and references to Appendices
PERNES CAMP	20/10/17	12.40pm	Remainder of Company paraded and moved off to PROVEN STATION.	
PROVEN STATION	"	1.30pm	The Company entrained for ST OMER	
ST. OMER	"	6.0pm	Company arrived and proceeded by march route to billets at OWERSTEL near WATTEN.	
OWERSTEL	"	8.30pm	The transport that proceeded by road arrived at H. ofr.	
— do —	21/10/17	10.15am	Company paraded for Divine Service and cleaning up billets.	
— do —	22/10/17	9.0am	Company paraded for drill and M. Gun Training.	
— do —	23/10/17	9.0am	ditto	
— do —	24/10/17	9.0am	Fatigue party of 30 men paraded for loading coal at WATTEN STATION.	
"	"	6.0am	Remainder of Company paraded for Drill and M. Gun Training.	
"	"	8.30am	Company paraded at billets with 8 " horse fighting limbers and proceeded to INGLINGHEM to attend the inspection of the Guards Division by the Commander in Chief.	
— do —	25/10/17	7.45am	Company paraded and B.Q.M. Stores moved to new billets at OUEST MONT	
— do —	"		Transport and B.Q.M. Stores moved to new billets at OUEST MONT	
OUEST MONT	"	2.30pm	Company arrived from inspection.	
— do —	26/10/17	8.30am	Company paraded for Drill, M. Gun Training and cleaning of billets.	
"	"		The D.T. Branic. Welsh Guards joined Company.	
— do —	27/10/17	8.45am	Company paraded for drill and M.Gun Training.	
— do —	28/10/17	10.0am	Divine Service.	
— do —	29/10/17	8.45am	Company paraded for Drill and Machine Gun Training. No.1 Section carried out Range Practices on Range at P.13.L. (Sh.27.A.S.E./200.06).	
— do —	30/10/17	8.15am	Company paraded and moved off to "D" range for firing.	
— do —	31/10/17	8.45am	Company paraded for Drill and M.Gun Training.	
— do —	"		Lieut V.G. North, Welsh Guards joined Company.	

In orders & reports during month.

1375 Sergt J. WILDE, Machine Gun Gds awarded the MILITARY MEDAL for operations on 9th and " 12th "
10.10 " 96 L. B WEATHERHEAD " " 13th "
914 " D. SWANSTON " " " "

[signatures]
Commanding M. Gun Coy.
3rd Gds Bde.

Army Form C. 2118

WAR DIARY
or
INTELLIGENCE SUMMARY
(Erase heading not required.)

For November 1917.

Place	Date	Hour	Summary of Events and Information	Remarks and references to Appendices
OUEST MONT	1-11-17	8.45ᴬᴹ	3rd Guards Brigade M. Gun Company. Company paraded for drill, machine gun training and range practice.	
"	2-11-17	7.45ᴬᴹ	Company paraded & by sections for baths at HOUTKERQUE. Captain Label-Smith MC left Company for 6 months light duty in England. Lt. F.A.T. Barlow temporarily took over command of Company.	
"	3-11-17	10.45ᴬᴹ	Company inspected by the Brigadier General.	
"	4-11-17	8.40ᴬᴹ	Company paraded for Divine Service at EPERLECQUES.	
"	5-11-17	8.45ᴬᴹ	Company paraded for drill, machine gun training and range practice. Inspection of rifles by Armourer Sergt. and inspection of the Appliances by Brigade Gas N.C.O.	
"	6-11-17	9.0ᴬᴹ	Company paraded and marched to INGLINGHEM to be inspected by General ANTHOINE Comdg 1st French Army. On arriving on the ground the inspection was cancelled and the Company returned to billets.	
"	7-11-17	8.30ᴬᴹ	Company paraded for drill, M.Gun Training and practice on miniature range.	
"	8-11-17	8.30ᴬᴹ	" " " " " " " "	
"	9-11-17	8.45ᴬᴹ	Company paraded and moved off by march route via THEROUANNE and ENQUIN to SERNY.	
SERNY	"	3.0ᴾᴹ	Company arrived in billets.	
"	10-11-17	11.45ᴬᴹ	Company paraded and moved by march route to LIVOSSART.	
LIVOSSART	"	3.0ᴾᴹ	Company arrived in billets.	
"	11-11-17	8.45ᴬᴹ	Company paraded and moved off by march route via HEUCHIN – WAVRANS – ST POL to HERLIN-LE-SEC.	
HERLIN-LE-SEC	"	4.0ᴾᴹ	Company arrived in billets.	
"	12-11-17	9.30ᴬᴹ	Company paraded in drill order for rifle inspection, and gunners clean fatigues dress for limber drill, afternoon cleaning guns, kit and billets.	
"	13-11-17	8.30ᴬᴹ	Company paraded for arm drill and rifle training.	
"	14-11-17	8.30ᴬᴹ	Company paraded for drill, Physical Training, Map Reading and judging distance.	
"	15-11-17	9.30ᴬᴹ	Company paraded in fighting order with fighting limbers and 2 Lim. Lambert to take part in Brigade Field Day. Dinners were eaten. Company returned to billets at 4.0ᴾᴹ

WAR DIARY or INTELLIGENCE SUMMARY

Army Form C. 2118

For month of November 1917 (Continued)

(Erase heading not required.)

Place	Date	Hour	Summary of Events and Information	Remarks and references to Appendices
HERILLE SEC	16.11.17	9.0 A/M	Company paraded for drill, M.Gun training and limber cleaning.	
"	17.11.17	8.30 A/M	Captain Johnstock joined Company from 4th Gds M.G. Company and took over command.	
"	"	1.0 P/M	Company paraded and moved off by march route via BUNEVILLE and HOUVIN-HOUVIGNEUL to OPPY.	
OPPY	"	2.30 A/M	Company arrived in billets.	
"	18.11.17		Company paraded and moved off by march route via SOMBRIN - SAULTY and TINCIES to BIENVILLERS-AU-BOIS.	
BIENVILLERS-AU-BOIS	"	4.0 P/M	Company arrived in billets.	
"	19.11.17	10.30 A/M	Company paraded for foot inspection.	
"	"	4.45 P/M	Company paraded and moved off by march route via BUCQUOY to ACHIET-LE-PETIT.	
ACHIET-LE-PETIT	"	8.0 P/M	Company arrived and accommodated in tents and huts.	
"	20.11.17	8.30 A/M	Company paraded for gas helmet inspection and general cleaning.	
"	21.11.17	9.0 A/M	Transport paraded and moved off to ROCQUIGNY.	
"	22.11.17	10 A/M	Company paraded and marched to ACHIET-LE-GRAND, there entraining for ROCQUIGNY.	
ROCQUIGNY	"	1.30 P/M	Company arrived and accommodated in huts.	
"	"	5.0 P/M	Company paraded and stench clothing properly cleaned.	
"	23.11.17	6.50 A/M	Company on marching order, and moved off to BEAUMETZ.	
BEAUMETZ	"	11.0 A/M	Company arrived and accommodated in tents.	
"	"	10.15 A/M	Company (less 3rd sub-section) paraded in fighting order with fighting limbers and marched to FLESQUIERES via GRAINCOURT.	
FLESQUIERES	24.11.17	3.0 A/M	Company arrived and accommodated in billets and dug-outs in rear of the Hindenburg Support Line.	
BEAUMETZ	"	7.30 A/M	Remainder of Transport and Q.M. Stores moved off for FLESQUIERES.	
FLESQUIERES	"	1.0 P/M	Transport to arrived and bivouacked about 500 yards outside FLESQUIERES.	
"	"	2.0 P/M	Lieutenant K.E.Edwards, Irish Guards proceeded to report to 2nd Bn. Scots Guards to find position for 4 machine guns. These were found as follows:—1 in LA JUSTICE FARM running North, 2 on the SUNKEN RD running from LA JUSTICE to GRAINCOURT, and 1 in reserve in front of a small copse 300 yards advance of the N.E. corner of FLESQUIERES.	
BOURLON SECTOR	"	11.30 P/M	Captain J.H.Stocks led the 4 guns and teams up to Batt. H.Q. 2nd Bn. Scots Guards and handed them over to Lt. K.E.Schwerdt.	

WAR DIARY or INTELLIGENCE SUMMARY

Army Form C. 2118

For month of November 1917 (Continued).

Place	Date	Hour	Summary of Events and Information	Remarks and references to Appendices
BOURLON SECTOR	24/11/17	10.30 p.m	In accordance with an order received from O.C. 2nd Bn. Scots Guards, 2nd Lt. K.E. Schweder went 2 guns with 2nd Bn. Scots Gds to BOURLON WOOD. Lt. Schweder remained behind with the other 2 guns and reported to O.C. 4 or 5 Bn. Grenadier Guards. 2/Lieut. J.C. Fraser, Grenadier Guards was ordered to report with 2 guns on night 24/25 to O.C. 2nd Bn. Scots Guards to proceed to BOURLON WOOD. O.C. 2nd Bn. Scots Guards therefore had 4 guns with him under 2/Lt. J.C. Fraser. Casualties, 1 O.R. wounded by M.G. fire.	
"	25/11/17	1.0 a.m	Lt. V.G. North relieved Lt. Schweder who was in support with 4 guns. Lt. Schweder left 2 of his guns in support and took 2 guns and teams from Lt. North and reported to O.C. 4 5th Bn. Grenadier Gds. at Bn. H.Q. at ANNEUX CHAPELLE.	
"	"	6.30 p.m	Lt. Schweder reported to O.C. 4 5 Bn. Grenadier Gds.	
"	"	9.0 p.m	The 2 guns and teams proceeded with the 4 5th Bn. Grenadier Gds. into BOURLON WOOD and took up a position at the S.W. corner of it.	
"	26/11/17	-	The Scots Gds. Guns team under Lieut. Fraser rendered very valuable assistance to the 2nd Bn. Scots Gds. and were highly recommended by the O.C. (Major Stirling). Casualties, 4 O.R. wounded and 1 O.R. missing.	
"	27/11/17	2.0 a.m	Lt. Schweder had orders that the 4 5 Bn. Grenadier Guards would take up a position in rear of the 2nd Bn Scots Guards who were to attack at 6.30 a.m. According to orders Scots Gds. Lt. Schweder took 2 guns and teams to BOURLON WOOD and mounted the guns on a hill situated near two old observation posts in a line due E. from the CHATEAUX in the centre of the wood with front facing FONTAINE - NOTRE - DAME. Casualties 1 O.R. Killed and 1 O.R. wounded.	
"	28/11/17	1.6 p.m	2 guns attacked to 4 Bn. Grenadier Gds. relieved by 2 guns under Sergt. W. Kelly and attached to 1st Bn. Welsh Gds. which relieved the 4 or 5 Bn. Grenadier Gds. in BOURLON WOOD. The 2 guns & teams relieved returned to Coy. H.Q. at FLESQUIERES.	
"	"	5.0 p.m	2/Lt. D.A. Davies with 2 guns and teams attached to the 1st Bn. Grenadier Guards proceeded to BOURLON WOOD and took up a position about 300 yards S.E. of the wood with front facing FONTAINE - NOTRE - DAME. During the night the 2 guns under 2/Lt. D.A. Davies and the 2 guns in support position under Lt. V.G. North were withdrawn and returned to Coy. H.Q. FLESQUIERES.	
"	29/11/17	8.30 a.m	The enemy commenced a big offensive.	
"	"	9.0 a.m	Captain W. Horkes, Scots Gds. Coy. officer giving the attack far the enemy came over the hill W. of BOURLON WOOD to Lt. Burbeck (O.M.(P.)) 15 Burbeck (O.M.(P.)) who immediately commenced and all round machine gun defence system of FLESQUIERES, as he had in the meantime	

WAR DIARY
INTELLIGENCE SUMMARY

For month of November 1917 (continued).

Army Form C. 2118

Instructions regarding War Diaries and Intelligence Summaries are contained in F.S. Regs., Part II. and the Staff Manual respectively. Title Pages will be prepared in manuscript.

(Erase heading not required.)

Place	Date	Hour	Summary of Events and Information	Remarks and references to Appendices
FLESQUIÈRES	29.11.17	9.0 p.m.	received information that the enemy had captured GOUZEAUCOURT and that he was pressing on behind. Accordingly 2nd Lt. J.C. Symes, 2nd Lt. V.G. North and 2nd Lt. D.A. Davis took up allotted positions round FLESQUIÈRES. 2nd Lt. K.E. Schneder was in reserve. 500 yards S. of the village.	
"	"	6.0 p.m.	Capt. M. Hockey received orders for the Company to retire on METZ-EN-COUTURE and rejoin the 3rd Guards Brigade who had left early on morning of the 29th.	
"	"	7.0 p.m.	Company paraded together with transport and moved off.	
METZ-EN-COUTURE	30.11.17	3.0 a.m.	Company arrived at B.H.Q. situated at Q 23 c sheet II Ewn Rex opposite. On arrival 2nd Lt. K.E. Schneder, 2nd Lt. V.G. North and 2nd Lt. D.A. Davis with 2 Guns and Teams each reported to H.Q. 2nd Bn. Scots Guards, H.Q. 1st Bn. Grenadier Guards and H.Q. 1st Bn. Grenadier Guards respectively. 2nd Lt. F.K. Fallows with Guards who had been attached to Company from 1yds M.G. Coy since 26th reported to H.Q. H.Q. Bn. Grenadier Guards to with Lt. Guns Teams. All teams took 2 day's rations with them. All Nine Teams co-operated with their respective Battalions on GONNELIEU. Transport and details bivouacked at G.B. 0:80. VALENCIENNES Sheet 17. 1/40000. Honours and Awards during month. Captain T.A. Tapp, M.C. Coldstream Guards, Arrived at Bn. to the MILITARY CROSS (This officer died of wounds on 31-10-17). No. 408 Pte. W. M.C. allister Machine Gun Corps, Awarded the MILITARY MEDAL.	

Mutchler
Capt.
Comdg. 3rd Guard's Bde. M. Gun Coy.

Army Form C. 2118.

WAR DIARY

For month of December 1917.

INTELLIGENCE SUMMARY.

(Erase heading not required.)

Instructions regarding War Diaries and Intelligence Summaries are contained in F. S. Regs., Part II. and the Staff Manual respectively. Title pages will be prepared in manuscript.

WO 25

Place	Date	Hour	Summary of Events and Information	Remarks and references to Appendices
			3rd Guards Brigade Machine Gun Company	
GOUZECOURT SECTOR	1-12-17	—	The following guns and teams in the line co-operated with Battalions to which attached on GONNE-LIEU. 2 Guns attached to 2nd Bn. Scots Guards. " 1st Bn. Welsh Guards. 2 " " 1st Bn. Grenadier Guards. 4 " " 4th Bn. Grenadier Guards. One section M.G. was kept in reserve to protect Northern end of GOUZECOURT against an expected attack by the enemy from direction of VILLERS PLOUICH.	
"	2-12-17	—	2/Lt. D.L. ROBISON, Scots Guards joined the Company.	
"	3-12-17	—	2/Lt. S.W. Bailey, Coldstream Guards joined the Company. Company relieved by 1st Gds. Bde. M. Gun Coy. Casualties during above period in the line - 5 O.R. killed & and 21 wounded.	
METZ-EN-COUTURE	4-12-17	—	Teams after being relieved in the line returned to Brigade at detail camp near METZ-EN-COUTURE (G.B. 02.80. VALENCIENNES Sheet 12. 1/40000). 2/Lt. F.K. Fallows, who has been temporarily attached to the Company from Division M. Gun Coy rejoined his unit.	
"	"	9.0 P.M	The whole Company paraded and moved off to ETRICOURT by march route via FINS.	
ETRICOURT	5-12-17	1.0 A.M	Company arrived and accommodated for the night in tents.	
"	"	7.30 A.M	Company's two transport paraded and entrained at ETRICOURT STATION for SAULTY. Q.M. Stores and blankets were conveyed on lorry.	
"	"	8.0 A.M	Transport paraded and moved off via LE TRASLOY to BEAULENCOURT	
"	"	12.30 P.M	Company arrived and detrained and proceeded by march route to BARLY.	
SAULTY	"	2.30 P.M	Company arrived and accommodated in huts. Officers Mess in farmhouse at BARLY.	
BARLY	"	1.30 P.M	Company arrived and remained above in M. Gun camp for a nights' rest.	
BEAULENCOURT	6-12-17	7.30 A.M	Transport paraded and continuing its march to BARLY.	
"	"	4.30 P.M	Transport paraded and move off via BAPAUME — BUCQUOY — POMMIER.	
BARLY	"		Transport arrived.	
"	7-12-17	9.30 A.M	Company paraded under Section arrangements for gun cleaning and kit-inspection.	
"	8-12-17	8.30 A.M	Company paraded for drill and physical training.	
"	"		2/Cpl. A.J. Burns attended at Gas course at XVII Corps School AGNEZ-LEZ-DUISAN.	
"	9-12-17	8.45 A.M	Company on Church parade for Divine Service.	

Army Form C. 2118.

WAR DIARY

For month of December 1917
(Continued).

INTELLIGENCE SUMMARY.

(Erase heading not required.)

Instructions regarding War Diaries and Intelligence Summaries are contained in F.S. Regs., Part II. and the Staff Manual respectively. Title pages will be prepared in manuscript.

Place	Date	Hour	Summary of Events and Information	Remarks and references to Appendices
BARLY	10-12-17	8.30 AM	Company paraded for arm drill, gas drill and stoppages.	
"	11-12-17	8.45 AM	Company paraded and moved off to ARRAS via FOSSEUX and BEAUMETZ.	
ARRAS.	"	1.0 PM	Company arrived and billetted in LEVIS BARRACKS. Officers mess in a civil residence in the Town.	
"	12-12-17	9.30 AM	Company paraded under section arrangements for lubrication, limber cleaning, stoppages, mechanism L-A.G., Blickburg gun and the 5th Rations received, the Company reconditioned the equipment and appointed from ARRAS to the line. Company warned to remain in billets from 7 AM to 9 AM daily. Sergt. P. Wilde and Officers attended Map reading and Bayonet fighting Courses respectively in the town at Brigade H.Q.	
"	13-12-17	9.0 AM	Company paraded for inspection of gas appliances followed by physical training and talk.	
"	14-12-17	9.15 AM	Company paraded under section arrangements for training. Gen. M.I. instrn.	
"	15-12-17	9.30 AM	Company paraded under section arrangements for P.T., Arm drill and M. Gun Training.	
"	16-12-17	9.0 AM	Company paraded under section arrangements for Divine Service. Instruction Classes fired at stoppages on MONT Range.	
			No. 33645 Pte K. Thornley in the Grenadier Gds. attached to Company awarded the MILITARY MEDAL.	
"	17-12-17	8.45 AM	Company paraded in drill order with greatcoats and marched to Range for practice. 8 Guns and 48 belt boxes being taken on limbers.	
"	18-12-17	8.45 AM	Company paraded for range practice as for previous day.	
"	19-12-17	7.30 AM	" bath, in clean fatigue dress	
		9.0 AM	" in drill order under section arrangements for gun Rk.inspection, belt filling	
		10.0 AM	Transport horses paraded for clipping which was carried out under the supervision of Lt V. Northy. Sergt. F. Hosking and 2/Cpl. E. Smith attended Map reading and Bayonet fighting Courses respectively at Brigade H.Q.	
"	20-12-17	8.30 AM	Company paraded for physical training followed by M.Gun Training with Sec. arrangements.	
"	21-12-17	9. AM	Company paraded for squad drill, gun drill, stoppages and belt filling.	
		9.30 AM	Barrack-room classes paraded and proceeded to ST. NICHOLAS Range to fire stoppages.	
"	22-12-17	8.30 AM	Company paraded in drill order with greatcoats and 2 guns and 6 belt boxes for section for range practice on MONT Range.	
"	23-12-17	9.0 AM	Company paraded for Divine Service.	
"	24-12-17	9.0 AM	Company paraded for M.G. Training. Barrack-room class paraded and proceeded to fire stoppages on ST. NICHOLAS Range.	

Army Form C. 2118.

WAR DIARY

INTELLIGENCE SUMMARY

For month of December 1917
(Continued).

(Erase heading not required.)

Instructions regarding War Diaries and Intelligence Summaries are contained in F. S. Regs., Part II. and the Staff Manual respectively. Title pages will be prepared in manuscript.

Place	Date	Hour	Summary of Events and Information	Remarks and references to Appendices
ARRAS	25-12-17	9.10am	Company paraded for Divine Service. 2/Lt. G.J. Jales M.G. Grenadier Guards awarded the MILITARY CROSS	
"	26-12-17	9.0am	Company paraded for physical training and drill. All Corporals paraded for instruction in Map reading by C.O.	
	10.0am	Instruction classes paraded for range practices on ST NICHOLAS Range. Signal course assembling at AGNES-LES-DUISANS. 1/Cpl. McBean proceded to Signal course	
"	27-12-17	9.0am	Company paraded in drill order with greatcoats for range practice. 1/Sgt. Wilson and 1/Cpl. H. Morgan attended Map reading and Bayonet fighting Course at Brigade HQ.	
"	28-12-17	8.30am	Company paraded for physical training and kit inspection followed by M.G. Training with section arrangements	
"	29-12-17	9.0am	Company paraded for range practices on WAILLY Range.	
"	30-12-17	9.0am	Company paraded for Divine Service.	
	3.0pm	Company paraded for Baths.	
"	31-12-17	8.30am	Company paraded for physical training for 1 hour followed by inspection of gas appliances. Beltfilling, gun and cleaning equipment carried out. Thursday Section arrangements.	

Mutung
Capt.
Comdg. 3rd Guard's Bde. M. Gun Coy.

B E F

GUARDS DIV

3 Gds Bde

3 Gds Bde Machine Gun Coy

1915 Dec to 1918 Feb

Guards Division
3rd Guards Brigade
3rd Machine Gun Coy.
Jan – Feb. 1918.

WAR DIARY

For month of January 1918 Army Form C. 2118.

Vol 26

INTELLIGENCE SUMMARY.

(Erase heading not required.)

Instructions regarding War Diaries and Intelligence Summaries are contained in F. S. Regs., Part II. and the Staff Manual respectively. Title pages will be prepared in manuscript.

Place	Date	Hour	Summary of Events and Information	Remarks and references to Appendices
			3rd Gds Brigade Machine Gun Company	
ARRAS	1-1-18	9.15 A.M	Company paraded and moved off to relieve the 46th Machine Gun Company with the left sector of Northern sector, XVII th Corps front. 13 Guns and Teams were found for the line as follows:—	
			Right Group, 4 guns. Centre Group, 4 guns. Left Group 4 guns. Reserve, 1 Gun. Remaining 3 guns to remain at Company Headquarters. Relief complete at 3 P.M.	
	"	11. 0 A.M	Company details and Remainder of transport not for the line paraded and moved off	
ST NICHOLAS	"	12.30 P.M	Details arrived.	
"	2-1-18	9. 0 A.M	Company details paraded at midnight orders for rifle and box respirator inspection, also at 10.30 A.M. for camp and Limbs cleaning	
"	3-1-18	"	Company details paraded for rifle inspection, run and gas drill.	
"	4-1-18	"	" Route march.	
"	5-1-18	"	Relieving Teams paraded and moved off for the line.	
"	6-1-18	10. 6 A.M	Details Camp paraded for inspection of equipment rifles and personal Kit.	
"	7-1-18	9. 0 A.M	" " box respirator inspection and physical training.	
"	8-1-18	"	" " arms drill and physical training.	
"	9-1-18	"	" " foot inspection and fuzz parade for men going into the line	
"	"	10.30 A.M	Relieving teams paraded and moved off for the line.	
"	10-1-18	11. 0 A.M	Details in camp paraded for inspection of equipment, rifles and personal Kit followed by pay parade for men proceeding on U.K. leave	
"	11-1-18	9. 0 A.M	Details in camp paraded for physical training, box respirator inspection followed by camp fatigue.	
"	12-1-18	9.30 A.M	Details in camp paraded for rifle inspection and camp fatigue.	
"	13-1-18	10.30 A.M	Relieving teams for the line paraded and moved off.	
"	14-1-18	11. 0 A.M	Details in camp paraded for inspection of rifles, equipment and personal Kit.	
"	15-1-18	9. 0 A.M	Details paraded for physical training and camp fatigue.	
"	16-1-18	9.30 A.M	Details in camp paraded for rifle inspection and camp fatigue.	
"	17-1-18	—	9 Guns and Teams in the line known as Northern Guns relieved by 2nd Gds Bde M Gun Coy.	
ARRAS	18-1-18	3. 0 P.M	Details arrived.	
"	"	4.30 P.M	Details paraded for transport moved to LEVIS BARRACKS, ARRAS.	

Army Form C. 2118.

WAR DIARY
or
INTELLIGENCE SUMMARY.

For month of January 1918 (Continued).

Instructions regarding War Diaries and Intelligence Summaries are contained in F. S. Regs., Part II. and the Staff Manual respectively. Title pages will be prepared in manuscript.

(Erase heading not required.)

Place	Date	Hour	Summary of Events and Information	Remarks and references to Appendices
ARRAS	18-1-18	—	Remaining 6 (Southern) guns in the line relieved by 2nd Gds Bde. M. Gun Company.	
"	19-1-18	10.0 A	Relief completed.	
"	19-1-18	10.0 A	Company less men relieved in the line paraded for rifle and box respirator inspection and at 10.30 for cleaning all guns and kit.	
"	20-1-18	9.15 A	Company paraded at 9. Divine Service.	
"	21-1-18	"	Company paraded for following work:— Inspection of gun kit, Transport fatigue, brickwork class, field firing on valley range, cleaning belts to be taken out from St Nicholas by N.5.Coy.	
"	22-1-18	8.0 A	Company paraded in drill order at Barracks for inspection of rifle etc. Party of 100 on parade. At 2.30 for fatigue at Transport. Brickwork classes carried out.	
"	23-1-18	8.30 A	Company paraded for range and gun drill at St. NICHOLAS.	
"	"	"	Company paraded for physical training and fatigue at Transport. Remainder paraded for kit and gas helmet inspection followed by preparing guns and kit for the line. Party paraded for fatigue at Transport.	
"	24-1-18	9.0 A		
"	25-1-18	2.0 P	Company relieved 6 guns of 2nd Gds Bde. M. Gun Coy. in right sector. Remainder paraded for arms drill fatigue and instruction.	
"	26-1-18	17.30	Remaining 10 guns and teams paraded for the line to complete relief of 2nd Gds Bde M.Gun Coy in right sector.	
"	"	2.0 A	Details paraded and moved off to St. NICHOLAS.	
ST NICHOLAS	27-1-18	9.6 A	" for arms drill and Transport fatigue	
"	28-1-18	"	" " " "	
"	29-1-18	"	" " " "	1 OR wounded on the line.
"	30-1-18	"	" " " "	

Honours & Awards during month :— No. 349 Sergt A.J. Baggs, Machine Gun Guards, awarded Croix de Guerre (Belgian).

Witherby
Capt.
Comdg. 3rd Guard's Bde. M. Gun Coy.

3rd Guards Brigade M.G. Coy

WAR DIARY for Month of February 1918.
Army Form C. 2118.

INTELLIGENCE SUMMARY

3rd Guards Brigade Machine Gun Company

Place	Date	Hour	Summary of Events and Information	Remarks and references to Appendices
ST NICOLAS	1-2-18	9. A.M.	Details paraded for Drill and Static fatigue.	
"	2-2-18	"	" " " " " "	
"	3-2-18	9.30 A	Details not for relief paraded for Camp fatigue.	
"	"	9.30 A	For relief paraded for rifle and gas Helmet inspection followed by foot rubbing.	
"	"	12 noon	Relief Teams with band moved off to relieve the teams in the line.	
"	4-2-18	8.30 A	Details paraded for fatigue at Transport lines.	
"	"	10.30 A	" relieved from the line paraded for inspection of rifles and box respirators	
"	5-2-18	8.30 A	" for fatigue at Transport lines and Backward Blond.	
"	"	1.15 P.M.	Officers out of the line attended a lecture on Intelligence at Bnd. HQ.	
"	6-2-18	8.30 A	Details paraded for fatigue at Transport lines	
"	"	9.6 P.M.	Backward Blond paraded for inspection.	
"	"	1.30 P.M.	All Details paraded and moved off to new quarters at LEVIS BARRACKS, ARRAS.	
ARRAS	"	2.30 P.M.	Details arrived at BARRACKS. Transport remained at ST NICOLAS.	
"	7-2-18	9.0 A	Details not for relief paraded for Backward Class and Barrack fatigue.	
"	"	9.30 A	" for relief paraded that the company were all about 11 a.m for foot rubbing and gas Helmet inspection.	
"	"	12.15 P.M	Relief paraded and moved off to relieve the teams in the line.	
"	8-2-18	9.0 A	Detail paraded for rifle, cap and clothing inspection followed by Arms Drill and Physical Training	
"	"	"	" Drill. Backward Class. Transport and Barrack fatigues.	
"	9-2-18	"	Lt. J. G. Jones. M.C. Guards proceeded to the Army S.O.S. School, FLIXECOURT for Infantry Course.	
"	10-2-18	9.35 A	Details paraded for Baths at ST NICOLAS	
"	"	—	" Bn'ses, Guards Furnish Company	
"	11-2-18	10.3 P	Detail for relief paraded for foot rubbing	
"	"	10.15 P	Relief paraded and moved off to relieve the teams in the line.	
"	12-2-18	10.6 A	Details paraded for rifle, L.G., clothing and Kit inspection.	
"	13-2-18	9.0 A	" for Arms Drills, cleaning of guns from line. Transport fatigue and Backward Class.	
"	14-2-18	9.0 A	" " " " " " "	

WAR DIARY for month of February 1918 (Contd)

Army Form C. 2118.

INTELLIGENCE SUMMARY

(Erase heading not required.)

Instructions regarding War Diaries and Intelligence Summaries are contained in F. S. Regs., Part II. and the Staff Manual respectively. Title pages will be prepared in manuscript.

Place	Date	Hour	Summary of Events and Information	Remarks and references to Appendices
ARRAS	15.2.18	9 A	Details handed in Drill Order for inspection of arms &c.	
"	"	9.30 A	" " for relief parades at 9.30 A for fatigues.	
"	"	10.30 A	" " for Relief parades for foot rubbing and inspection of Gas appliances	
"	"	12.15 P	Relief paraded and moved off to relieve 6 and on the line.	
"	16.2.18	9 A	Details paraded for Barrack fatigues and Backwork Class.	
"	"	10 A	" " Relieved from the line paraded for rifle, cap & clothing inspection followed by Kit inspection.	
"	17.2.18	9 A	" " paraded for Arms Drill, Backwork Class, Transport & Barrack fatigue.	
"	18.2.18	9 A	" " " " " "	
"	19.2.18	9 A	" in Drill Order for inspection of arms &c.	
"	"	9.30 A	" " for relief parades at 9.30 A for fatigues.	
"	"	10.30 A	" " for Relief parades for foot rubbing and inspection of Gas appliances	
"	"	12.15 P	Relief paraded and moved off to relieve & on the line.	
"	20.2.18	9 A	Details paraded for Backwork Class, Transport & Barrack fatigue.	
"	"	10 A	" " relieved from the line paraded for rifle, cap and clothing inspection followed by Kit inspection.	
"	21.2.18	9 A	" Sunday, Gal. Church parade at 9 A join'd Coy parade.	
"	"	10 A	Details paraded at 9 A for Arms Drill, Backwork Class, Transport & Barrack fatigue.	
"	22.2.18	9 A	" " " " " "	
"	23.2.18	9 A	" in Drill Order for inspection.	
"	"	9.30 A	" " for relief paraded for Barrack & Transport fatigue.	
"	"	12.15 P	Relief paraded and moved off for the line.	
"	24.2.18	9.30 A	Details paraded for Transport fatigue.	
"	"	10 A	" " returned from the line paraded for rifle, Cap & Clothing inspection followed by Kit inspection.	
"	25.2.18	10.45 A	Dom. E. Service for the encampments.	
"	"	9 A	Details paraded for Arms Drill, Transport & Barrack fatigue.	
"	26.2.18	9 A	" " " " " "	
"	27.2.18	9 A	" " " " " "	
"	"	10 A	" in Drill Order for inspection.	
"	"	9.30 A	" " for relief paraded for Barrack and Transport fatigue.	
"	"	10.30 A	" " for Relief paraded for foot rubbing and inspection of gas appliances.	
"	"	12.15 P	Relief paraded and moved off for the line.	
"	28.2.18	9 A	Details paraded for Backwork Class & fatigue.	
"	"	10.30 A	" " have had for inspection followed by bath.	

M.G.B.
1-3-18

[signature] Lt.
Comd'g 3— Gen Base M.G. Coy.

Guards Division.
3rd Gds Brigade
Machine Gun Coy.
Jan — Dec 1917.

www.ingramcontent.com/pod-product-compliance
Lightning Source LLC
Chambersburg PA
CBHW081449160426
43193CB00013B/2421